REDBACK QUARTERLY 8

ECONOBABBLE

HOW TO DECODE POLITICAL SPIN AND ECONOMIC NONSENSE

Richard Denniss

Published by Redback Quarterly,
an imprint of Schwartz Publishing Pty Ltd
Level 1, 221 Drummond Street
Carlton VIC 3053, Australia
enquiries@blackincbooks.com
www.redbackquarterly.com.au

National Library of Australia Cataloguing-in-Publication entry:
Denniss, Richard, author.
Econobabble: how to decode political spin and economic nonsense /
Richard Denniss.
9781863958042 (paperback)
9781925203806 (ebook)
Policy sciences—Australia. Politics, Practical—Australia.
Australia—Politics and government.
Australia—Economic policy.
320.994

Cover design by Peter Long
Cover illustration by Arthur Saron Sarnoff
Typesetting by Tristan Main

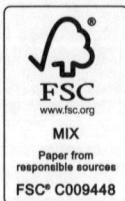

FSC
www.fsc.org
MIX
Paper from
responsible sources
FSC® C009448

Printed in Australia by Griffin Press. The paper
this book is printed on is certified against
the Forest Stewardship Council® Standards.
Griffin Press holds FSC chain of custody
certification SGS-COC-005088. FSC promotes
environmentally responsible, socially beneficial
and economically viable management of the
world's forests.

CONTENTS

INTRODUCTION
WHAT IS ECONOBABBLE?

*'If I turn out to be particularly clear, you've probably
misunderstood what I've said.'*
—ALAN GREENSPAN, FORMER GOVERNOR
OF THE US FEDERAL RESERVE

Economics is like a tyre lever: it can be used to
solve a problem, or to beat someone over the
head. It's not the tyre lever that is good or bad –
it's the person who wields it, and what they try
to do with it.

Economics has some simple but powerful analytical
tools that can be used to support both good and bad ideas.
It also has a powerful language that can conceal simple
truths from the public. I call this language econobabble,
and it includes two things: incomprehensible economic
jargon, and apparently simple words that have been
stripped of their normal meanings. When public figures
and commentators use this sort of language in order to
dress up their self-interest as the national interest, to
make the absurd seem inevitable or the inequitable seem

fair, or even to make the destructive seem prudent, they are econobabbling.

Every day, econobabble silences democratic debate about our nation's priorities and values, and conceals the policy options that we have at our disposal. The aim of this book is to expose the stupid arguments, bizarre contradictions and complete lack of evidence which econobabble is designed to conceal.

I am sorry to say it, but in our nation today confidence is usually more important than qualifications. Bad economic arguments without the faintest theoretical or empirical foundation dominate public debate. And when nonsense is repeated often enough – especially by well-paid lobbyists, commentators and businesspeople – it can start to seem as though everyone believes that black is white, or up is down. After enough exposure to econobabble, you might even come to think that the best way to help poor people is to give tax cuts to the rich.

This book won't train you as an economist. (Given the lack of qualifications of most people who spout econobabble, however, that shouldn't worry you too much.) But it will give you the evidence, the arguments and, most importantly, the confidence to question assertions you might once have simply accepted, or lacked the confidence to challenge.

This book is for those who, deep down, have never believed that it makes sense, economic or otherwise, to help poor people by slashing public spending on the services they rely on. It's for those who have a sneaking suspicion that it would be cheaper to avoid climate change than to let it happen and then 'adapt'. And it's for those who think it would be more efficient to reduce unemployment than to ship jobs offshore. It will show you how to take on those who pride themselves on being 'great economic managers' but then do nothing more than blame the un-employed for the lack of jobs.

I'm not trying to convince you that economics is stu-pid – I don't think it is. But I am trying to convince you to join the fight against people who use econobabble to con-ceal their self-interest. Just as you don't need a black belt in karate to call out bullying when you see it, you don't need an economics degree to call out bullshit when you hear it. Until enough of us name econobabble for what it is, our public debate will never have room for good ideas based on evidence, logic and our collective values.

CHAPTER 1
THE LANGUAGE OF DECEPTION

Before taking on the role of 'managing the Australian economy', Malcolm Turnbull was a lawyer. Tony Abbott dabbled in journalism and the priesthood, Ben Chifley was an engine driver and John Howard was a suburban solicitor. Paul Keating managed a rock band. You do have to be a lawyer to become attorney-general, but you don't have to be an economist to be the prime minister. Indeed, you don't even have to be an economist to be the treasurer.

Although most politicians have no training in economics, and sometimes lack even the most superficial knowledge of how the Australian economy works, they are often highly skilled in using economic language to bamboozle or silence the public. They use words like *productivity* when they mean *profit*. They say things like 'The economy is overheated' when they mean 'The wages of low-paid workers are growing faster than I think they should'. Words matter.

Economics is far more complicated than political slogans such as 'Repay the debt' suggest. Questions such as 'Should we have a deficit or shouldn't we?' don't have a simple answer. And economics is far less capable of predicting the future than the politicians and bureaucrats who spend mountains of taxpayers' money on flawed 'forecasts' would care to admit.

Catholic priests used to say mass in Latin, knowing full well that their mostly uneducated audiences had little idea what was being said. But the purpose of such sermons was not to explain or persuade. The purpose was to silence. How can you disagree with something you don't understand?

Economists often speak in Latin and Ancient Greek. We love to wear folk down with a few *deltas* and *gammas*, before finishing them off with a bit of *ceteris paribus*. One of our best tricks is to use words that sound like English but which have very specific meanings in the field of economics. We use simple-sounding words like *efficiency* and *unemployment* to draw the unsuspecting in. Then, when they admit to thinking that unemployment is measured by the number of people on the dole (it's not), or to thinking that efficiency means reducing waste (not to economists, it doesn't), we slam the door on their fingers.

To be clear, I'm not suggesting for a minute that only economists should be allowed to be prime minister or treasurer, or to run a business. That would be as dangerous as it is undemocratic. My point is that the vast majority of people who talk confidently about 'what the economy needs' have no more knowledge of economics than the average citizen. What they possess is confidence, not credentials.

The primary purpose of the econobabble that fills our airwaves is to keep ordinary Australians out of the big debates about tax, fairness, climate change and the provision of essential services. Like the congregation at a Latin mass, they can't follow what the high priests are saying. And that's just the way politicians and so-called business leaders like it.

ECONOMICS IS MORE FREQUENTLY USED TO CONCEAL THAN TO REVEAL

Using econobabble is a terrible way to encourage a productive public debate. But it's a great way to stifle one, and to confound and confuse Australians. That's the reason we hear so much of it.

Like any discipline, economics has its own professional language – jargon – which can be used either to speed up conversations between experts or to keep the uninitiated out of their deliberations. When non-economist politicians use economic jargon while talking to non-economist voters, you can be pretty certain what their objective is.

Just as a patient having a heart attack in an emergency ward is unlikely to understand what the doctors are saying to each other, so too someone listening to two economists argue about the relative strength of monetary policy transmission mechanisms will miss the significance of much is what is said. But a good doctor also knows how to use an entirely different vocabulary to explain to the patient what happened, what was done about it, and what it all means for the patient's future.

Anyone who really understands their subject matter can explain it to someone else. *If* they really understand it. And if they really want the other person to understand it too.

Like economics itself, jargon isn't dangerous. But econobabble is used to limit the menu of democratic choices that we are offered. Politicians rely on it to make themselves seem smart and to make the public feel dumb. The strategy has worked a treat for the last few decades.

WHAT THE HELL IS THE HANG SENG?

If elected leaders are to tackle big problems on our behalf, we need them to identify those problems clearly, explain the different options for fixing or ignoring the problem, and build a case for their preferred response. It's simple stuff, and it is the opposite of relying on econobabble to conceal problems, options and consequences.

But it is not just the politicians who need to change. Policy advocates, the media and the voting public all have to admit some simple truths. Let's start with an easy one: almost no one knows what the Hang Seng Index is.

The Hang Seng is an indicator of the financial performance of the companies listed on Hong Kong's stock exchange, which is Asia's third-largest. Almost no Australians know that, or care. And we can be pretty sure that anyone who does actually know about such things will not be tuning in to the nightly television news to find out what happened to their investments that day. So why do television stations waste their time on such indicators each night?

Presumably for the same reason that economists speak in Latin. The Hang Seng – and other similar indexes, such as the ASX 200, the Nikkei and the Dow Jones – are there to remind every night us that there is much we don't understand. Its role is to silence, not to inform.

MARKETS DON'T HAVE FEELINGS – RICH PEOPLE HAVE FEELINGS

The overwhelming majority of Australians think that we should spend more money on health, education and public transport. The vast majority of us also believe that Apple, Google and Gina Rinehart should pay more tax.[1] Nearly everyone agrees that big corporations should be banned from donating money to political parties. We live in a democracy, yet the fact that most of us want these changes is not sufficient to achieve them. 'Business leaders' tell us that we can only consider such changes after we 'consult the markets'.

Like the gods of cultures past, the markets can be angry. They can be vengeful. And they can punish non-believers. We must consult them cautiously. Tony Abbott once supported holding an inquiry into the impact of mining companies' decisions to double their iron ore production on the price of iron ore. However, a week later, after pressure from those same mining companies, he told us that to even inquire into the fall in the iron ore price might spook the markets, and stated that 'the last thing this government would ever want to do is interfere with a free market like the iron ore market'. Especially after they tell us not to, it seems.[2]

While markets are real, it is absurd to suggest that they have 'feelings', 'needs' or 'demands'. Markets are a place where buyers and sellers of a product come together. It might be a physical place like a fish market, or a virtual place like eBay or a stock exchange. But regardless of their form, markets never have feelings.

Rich people, on the other hand, do have feelings. And rich people who own billions of dollars' worth of shares in a company often have very strong feelings. They have feelings about government policies and they have feelings about tax rates.

But the feelings of rich people are quite different to the feelings of 'the market'. Consider the following example, which shows how effectively economic language can conceal what's actually going on. Both the following reports describe the same event:

> Markets reacted angrily today to news the government is considering tightening thin capitalisation provisions, which have provided foreign investors with strong incentives to expand their Australian operations.

> Rich foreigners reacted angrily today at news that they might have to pay tax on the profits they earn in Australia. After the government announced that it was considering clamping down on some of the most lucrative forms of multinational profit-shifting, some very wealthy Americans threatened to take their businesses away from Australia if they were forced to pay tax.

Words matter.

Governments and citizens alike should be concerned about the impact of changes in government policy on businesses. But the notion that Australia, one of the richest countries the world has ever known, can't change its laws without consulting with 'the market' is as absurd as it is alarming. In effect, we are we regularly being told by our own leaders that Australia can't change its laws unless some very rich people, most of whom live in other countries, say it's okay for us to do so.

The trick only works when, like a monster in a horror

movie, 'the market' seems close enough to be threatening but not so close that we can see it is made of papier-mâché. The vague, lurking but formless presence of 'the market' is far more ominous than reports about what happened to the weighted average price of shares in south-east Asian stock exchanges today (AKA the Hang Seng).

The nightly news gives us a regular reminder that 'the market' is watching and judging us. It might seem common sense that if we collected more tax, as they do in Norway, we could have health and education systems just as good as Norwegians have. But econobabble limits the options in front of us. 'What? You want to spend more money on health and education? Just imagine how the market would react to such a suggestion! You must be mad!'

Of course, in reality the market doesn't *want* anything. The market doesn't judge us, or anybody. The market is a metaphor, and it can no more judge our actions than Zeus or Apollo. The really scary question is whether or not the people going on about 'market sentiment' know this. As the saying goes, the best patsy doesn't know they are a patsy.

Whether the econobabblers are talking about 'what the markets want' or 'what the economy needs' or what a 'responsible government must do', their language and metaphors are systematically used to limit the range of options that are 'sensible' or 'pragmatic' or (most frequently) 'responsible'. Consider the following statements, both of which convey the same economic information:

- The budget deficit has grown rapidly in the last three years, even as the economy has grown strongly.

- Over the last three years the government has invested heavily in the new infrastructure that rapid economic growth requires.

Just as there is nothing 'irresponsible' or 'unsustainable' about an individual borrowing to buy a house, or a company borrowing to invest in a profitable new project, there is nothing irresponsible about a government borrowing to invest in the infrastructure that a rapidly growing population and economy need.

But for someone who would prefer to see governments collect less tax from him or herself and spend less money on others, droning on about the way that taxes 'destroy incentive' or about how welfare payments 'discourage work' sounds a lot less selfish, and is far more effective politically, than stating the simple truth. As J.K. Galbraith once said, 'The modern conservative is engaged in one of man's oldest exercises in moral philosophy; that is, the search for a superior moral justification for selfishness.'

HOW TO DECODE ECONOBABBLE

There are four simple rules you can use to decode the jargon that politicians and businesspeople so frequently use to keep the public out of the public debate:

- Ask them to say it again in English. If they know what they are talking about, that won't be hard.

- Listen carefully, and get them to clarify what key words mean to them (for instance, the meaning of a word like *efficiency* often varies greatly depending on who's using it). Again, people who know what they are talking about and have nothing to hide won't mind explaining what they mean by terms like *efficiency* or *competitive*.

- Ask them if their strong opinions about how parts of the economy work are based on evidence or simply 'gut feel'. It's one thing to 'know' that tax cuts will make rich people work harder and thus increase the incomes of poor people, but it's another thing altogether to have evidence. (Hint: some of the richest countries in the world with the lowest unemployment have high taxes. Northern Europe does exist.)

- Walk away when they start talking in generalities about 'supply and demand' or 'market forces'. Blaming 'the law of demand' for an economic outcome is like blaming the law of gravity for a plane crash – it's proof that the speaker has no idea what they are talking about, or no intention of explaining their thinking to you.

Too often we have allowed ourselves to be spoken down to by those who seek to serve us. It's time we demanded better. In the following chapters we'll look at a number of important policy areas in which econobabble is everywhere:

climate change, unemployment, debt and the budget, the free market and free trade. We'll also look at the business of economic modelling, and how it's regularly used to deceive. Finally, we'll consider what can be done.

My hope is that this book will empower you to call out the bullshit when you hear it.

CHAPTER 2
TACKLING CLIMATE CHANGE

It takes a flood of econobabble to convince people that it would be cheaper and better to cause climate change than to prevent it. But a flood we have had.

The mining companies that shed tens of thousands of workers the moment new technology allowed it – the same companies that are developing robot trucks and trains so they can sack their drivers – thunder away about the need to 'protect jobs'. Not since menthol cigarettes were marketed as a 'healthy option' has an industry been so audacious in its hypocrisy. When the coal industry in the Hunter Valley switched from underground mining to open-pit mining, it shed 20,000 jobs. When the Kennett government privatised Victoria's electricity generators, the new owners shed 10,000 jobs.[1]

Sitting just behind the ridiculous claim that causing climate change is good because it creates jobs is plenty of econobabble. Terms such as 'least cost abatement', 'discount rate', 'abatement cost curve' and 'network stability' help these industry lobbyists make the inexplicable seen inevitable.

A millennium's worth of common sense that 'an ounce of prevention is better than a pound of cure' and that 'a stitch in time saves nine' has somehow been transformed into the modern conventional wisdom: 'Let's just let things rip and assume that, in the future, someone will invent a solution for the problems we're causing.' The fact that people who call themselves 'conservatives' are driving this radical new approach to risk makes their rhetorical and political achievement all the more remarkable.

The biggest and most cynical hoax of modern political life is the assertion that tackling climate change will be 'expensive' and 'harmful to the economy'. On the contrary, it will save us a lot of money in the short term, and will save us from permanently altering the climate in the long run. It won't 'hurt the economy' or 'upset the markets', but it might hurt the bank balances of those who own hundreds of billions of dollars' worth of shares in coal, oil and gas, or in investments dependent on them. The truth is that tackling climate change can't 'cost jobs' in any economy-wide sense. Investment in new technologies creates jobs in the short term, and increases productivity in the long term.

Some billionaires have spent decades, and a lot of money, telling us that dealing with climate change will hurt the poor, and that causing it will help them. It's not the fact that these people would lie to protect their interests that is surprising – it's that anyone else takes them seriously.

Malcolm Turnbull once claimed that blocking the construction of the enormous Adani-Carmichael mine in Queensland's Galilee Basin would not make 'one iota' of difference to global greenhouse gas emissions, yet simultaneously claimed that blocking the same mine would prevent poor people in developing countries from gaining access to affordable energy.[2] Let's break that claim down into its component parts.

The first part of the prime minister's claim – that building new supply capacity in Australia has no impact on global supply and global consumption – makes no economic sense. First-year economics tells us that building new mines increases the supply of coal, pushes down the price and, in turn, leads to an increase in the quantity consumed. And it's not just the economic textbooks that predict this sequence of events. Ivan Glasenberg, the CEO of Glencore, the world's largest coal trading company, has repeatedly made the same observation.[3]

But let's assume that Prime Minister Turnbull is right when he suggests that building new coal mines doesn't lead to an increase in the amount of coal supplied. If that were the case, and new coal production in Australia simply displaced coal production in another country, then how could building new mines help to provide the additional energy required to lift millions of people out of energy poverty?

While logic dictates that Australian coal could *either* displace overseas coal production *or* add to world production to help lift poor people out of 'energy poverty', econobabble allows Australian coal production to do both at the same time!

Econobabble is a powerful tool, especially when used by the rich and powerful.

BLACK IS WHITE, UP IS DOWN AND THE MAIN GOAL OF MINING COMPANIES IS TO HELP THE POOR

The climate change debate is not a fight about science – it is a fight about economics and politics. There are few 'climate sceptics' in countries that don't have large fossil-fuel industries. The Australian media don't take fluoride sceptics or vaccination sceptics seriously – but there isn't a lot of money to be made out of bad teeth and sick kids.

'Climate sceptics' and the economic 'experts' who back them up have a few favoured talking points:

- Doing something about climate change would cost thousands of jobs.

- We can't afford schools and hospitals without all the tax paid by the mining industry.

- A carbon tax would destroy our exports and ruin our economy.

Fossil-fuel companies and their lobbyists trot out these arguments at every opportunity in order to justify ignoring the findings of the world's scientific community. In this chapter we will take each argument in turn. But before we decode the econobabble used by the polluters, we should understand a few important truths.

SUBSIDIES CAUSE CLIMATE CHANGE, AND REMOVING THEM WOULD SAVE GOVERNMENTS A FORTUNE

Climate change is primarily caused by the burning of fossil fuels, and coal is the single biggest source of greenhouse gas emissions in the world.[4] All the coal mined in Australia is heavily subsidised by governments. Indeed, governments around the world, over the past century, have spent hundreds of billions of taxpayer dollars building coal mines, coal-fired power stations, and the ports and railways needed to transport coal. Taxpayers even paid for the very long, expensive and inefficient power lines that connect remote power stations to cities, where most of the energy is used.

Attending a public school in Australia is cheap because the state and federal governments pick up most of the costs, and the same is true for 'cheap' coal. According to the Queensland budget papers, between 2008–09 and 2013–14 the taxpayers of that state spent $9.5 billion to build infrastructure needed by the coal mining industry.[5]

While the industry argues that taxpayer-provided coal loaders aren't a subsidy, the Queensland Treasury disagrees: 'Governments face budget constraints, and spending on mining-related infrastructure means less infrastructure spending in other areas, including social infrastructure such as hospitals and schools.'[6]

Everyone knows that 'coal is cheap', but few realise it is so cheap because of all the government support it has received over the past century. Imagine if you approached the government and proposed that you would build a hotel in a beautiful remote location. 'Foreign tourists will love it,' you say, 'and it will create jobs for the local Indigenous population. All I need is for the government to build me a port, an airport, an access road, an electricity supply, a water supply and a sewerage treatment works.' Having convinced the government to do all that, imagine that you were then able to persuade the public that you hadn't received any subsidies at all! Econobabble is a powerful tool.

Between 2008 and 2014 Australian state governments gave $17.6 billion in subsidies to the mining industry.[7] The states have paid to build roads, rail lines, ports, electricity supplies and water treatment facilities. There is no doubt that the costs of all these projects are public subsidies to private companies, and they make the price of coal and other minerals artificially cheap.

According to its own budget papers, in 2013–14 the West Australian government spent more money on infrastructure for the mining and gas industries ($1.4 billion) than it did on police ($1.2 billion). That year, too, New South Wales spent almost the same amount on its mining industry ($136 million) as it did on its Environmental Protection Authority ($138 million), which is supposed to oversee the mining industry. South Australia did worse still: $71 million to the miners, and just $49 million to its EPA.[8]

The fact that the miners say they couldn't operate without such support is proof that they are subsidies. Only the econobabble of 'investment in multi-use infrastructure' has insulated the mining industry from scrutiny. But we should ask the question: why, of all the infrastructure which we as taxpayers could build, should we start with the projects that private mining companies need?

WOULD YOU LIKE FREE COAL WITH THAT?

It gets worse. While car companies have to buy the steel they need to make cars, and bakers have to buy the flour they need to make bread, coal miners sometimes get 'their' coal for free. A decision by a government to give free coal to coal miners might be a bit hard to explain, and that's where econobabble comes in.

In order to 'encourage' (subsidise) the construction of new coal mines in Queensland's Galilee Basin, the former LNP state government led by Campbell Newman proposed a 'royalty ramp-up' or a 'royalty holiday' for the mines. How nice! Who wouldn't want a holiday in Queensland? But what does it actually mean?

Royalties are the price that miners pay for the resources they take from the ground. The term relates to the fact that the Crown (or the Queen's governments, in Australian states) owns the minerals our nation's land contains. In *The Beverly Hillbillies*, the Clampett family profited from the oil they discovered on their land, but in Australia it's the state, not the landholder, that gets rich from our underground wealth. At least, that's the theory.

The details of Campbell Newman's offer to the Galilee coal miners were so opaque that it's hard to put an exact figure on his generosity, but if we apply the usual royalty per tonne in Queensland to the 350 million tonnes of coal which the Carmichael mine plans to produce in its first ten years, the 'royalty holiday' (free coal) could have been worth as much as $1 billion.

Of course, the miners say that a royalty holiday isn't a subsidy. But if Campbell Newman gave them free rent for their headquarters in Brisbane, that would be a subsidy. And if he gave them free electricity or free water, that would be a subsidy too. But apparently giving them free coal isn't a subsidy – it's an 'investment'. In the words of the Galilee Basin Development Strategy, getting free coal is 'recognition of the significant up-front capital expenditure costs for first movers'. Econobabble at its best. By the way, miners often get free water as well.

The willingness of governments – not just recently, and not just in Australia – to use taxpayers' money to 'develop' the coal industry, and then, having done so, to give the coal away for free or at heavily discounted prices, is one of the major reasons that coal is considered to be such a 'cheap' form of energy. Cars would be cheap if taxpayers paid for the car factories and gave car companies free steel. And bread would be cheap if taxpayers funded bread factories and gave the bakers free wheat.

When taxpayers support industries other than mining, it's acknowledged as a subsidy. And in recent decades, the conservative governments that love subsidising the mining industry have raged against the provision of subsidies to the textile, automotive and other industries. Hypocrisy on such a scale can only survive under a thick coating of econobabble.

BUT WITHOUT FREE INFRASTRUCTURE AND FREE COAL WE WON'T BUILD NEW MINES!

Exactly.

In recent decades, those seeking to respond to the scientific warnings about the catastrophic consequences of climate change have expended enormous personal and political energy pushing for carbon taxes and emissions trading schemes. And there is no doubt these policies are sensible and potentially beneficial. But what is unclear is why the strategists behind the global push for climate action focused so much effort on the hard task of introducing a new tax, and so little on the historically easier task of opposing taxpayer subsidies for unpopular industries.

The mining industry is adamant that it wouldn't or couldn't mine as much coal without the enormous taxpayer support it receives. That's great to know. If the miners are telling the truth about this, then Australia can significantly reduce its greenhouse gas emissions by doing nothing more than ending its mining subsidies. And the money which is saved can be spent on health and education – areas that voters want to be funded better. That doesn't sound too scary or too economically harmful, does it?

But what if the miners are lying, and ending the subsidies doesn't stop them from mining at all? Well, if that's the case, then why should governments continue giving them billions of dollars? If we scrap the subsidies and the miners keep mining, then our governments can spend the spare tens of billions of dollars on health and education – or perhaps on non-polluting forms of energy production such as solar or wind.

Put simply, it takes a lot of taxpayer money to make coal 'cheap'. Removing the infrastructure subsidies to miners will save taxpayers a fortune. Ensuring the miners pay a fair royalty for the coal they take from our ground will raise another fortune. And if the result of filling the government's coffers with all of that money is an increase in coal prices and a reduction in coal consumption … well, that's even better.

ECONOMISTS AREN'T THE ONLY ONES WHO MAKE SIMPLISTIC ASSUMPTIONS

Courses in introductory economics rely on a highly simplified concept known as 'perfect competition'. In the imaginary world of perfect competition, lots of small producers trade with lots of customers, no one has any market power, consumers are rational, sellers are honest, and there are no advantages from mass production (or 'economies of scale', if you want to sound like an economist).

It makes sense to start teaching economics with a simplified model like this. But it doesn't make sense to apply it to real-world problems. And this is what many economists and policy-makers do when they try to force a complex reality to fit a simple model. To a man with a hammer, the whole world looks like a nail.

Unfortunately, most environmentalists, scientists and politicians who advocate for better climate policy have made a similar error: they have assumed that the market for coal is working relatively well, and that it only suffers from one 'market failure' in the form of the pollution costs that are ignored by miners and by power station owners. (If you call these *external costs* or *externalities*, you can really start to sound like an economist.)

If the market for coal was 'perfectly competitive', then there would be no price distortions, no market power and no subsidies, and introducing a carbon price would be a logical policy if we wanted to reduce the pollutions that cause climate change. But of course the coal market isn't perfectly competitive – not by a long shot. So while theory might say that introducing a carbon price is the best way to reform the industry and reduce pollution, in reality eliminating subsidies makes more economic sense (and far more political sense).

Unfortunately, too many environmentalists and economists have failed to recognise that the coal industry is so heavily subsidised. Their idealistic view of the coal market has meant that, rather than focusing on the subsidies given to coal mines, oil exploration and coal-fired electricity generators, they have tried to educate the population about science and build support for a new tax. Science is hard and taxes are rarely popular, and so the strategy hasn't worked very well so far.

The reason the mining industry is fighting so hard to deny that it is heavily subsidised proves the importance of removing its subsidies. In a perfectly competitive world a carbon tax makes a lot of sense, but in the messy world we have created for ourselves, abolishing the subsidies the miners rely on is not only the most efficient way to start tackling climate change, it will also be the cheapest and the most popular.

DECODING THE ECONOBABBLE USED TO SUPPORT CLIMATE INACTION

The best way to win an argument with the polluters is to highlight the internal contradictions in their arguments.

The miners say they can't live without subsidies, while the conservatives say they don't believe in giving out subsidies, so it shouldn't be hard to win such a fight. But it is. People with billions of dollars invested in pollution-causing industries are not going to walk away from our money without a battle.

The first thing we should understand is that the polluters themselves do not believe the arguments they use to support their industry. The polluters have spent a lot of time and money testing and developing arguments that are designed to be persuasive, or at least challenging, for progressive and centrist voters. That's why companies that want to abolish unfair-dismissal laws always say they are worried about 'protecting jobs', and why those who want to profit from causing climate change argue that environmentalists don't care about the poor.

Let's take a closer look at their main arguments.

1. Doing something about climate change would cost thousands of jobs.

That's correct – it will. Any significant change must result in some workers and capitalists losing out. Ending the whaling industry cost whalers their jobs. Ending asbestos mining cost asbestos workers their jobs. The invention of the digital camera destroyed the jobs of photo development lab workers.

According to the Australian Bureau of Statistics, between 1998 and 2009 the average monthly inflow to the pool of employed people was 372,000, and the average monthly outflow was 368,000. The result, then, of this enormous amount of 'churn' in the labour market was that total employment grew by just 4000 jobs per month.[9] The labour market is more like a swirling river than a still pond, and people change their jobs all the time, despite the enormous personal, family, community, social and economic costs.

The sick joke, however, is that the industries and political parties making the most noise about 'protecting jobs' from policies that aim to tackle climate change are the same voices who want to make it easier for companies to sack workers, and harder for the unemployed to get unemployment benefits.

Involuntary job losses are devastating, but it is clear that whether or not we tackle climate change, there will be involuntary job losses. Lots of them. Thirty years ago manufacturing accounted for 17 per cent of employment in Australia. Today it is 8 per cent. One hundred and ten years ago agriculture accounted for about 30 per cent of employment in Australia. Today it is 3 per cent. The conservative commentators who feign concern about jobs in mining never mourn the loss of manufacturing jobs.[10]

The collapsing world price of coal in 2014–15 led to some 10,000 jobs going in the coal mining industry. The carbon tax is gone, the mining tax is gone and 10,000 mining jobs have gone anyway.[11] The idea that the best way to reduce unemployment in Australia is to cause climate change is ridiculous.

What drove the world price of coal down that led to the job losses in coal mining? The massive expansion in Australia's coal mine construction, which was based on overly optimistic forecasts of how much coal the Chinese and Indians would want to buy from us. (By the way, have you noticed how those in the mining industry blame the job losses on the Chinese for not buying enough coal, rather than on us for producing too much coal? How's that for brilliant econobabble.)

Tony Abbott's 2013 declaration that, if elected to government, he would cut 20,000 jobs from the public sector is clear proof that some jobs are less important than others.[12] But if jobs in the public sector are the least important (to politicians talking about jobs, at least), then the coal mining industry must take the biscuit for having the most politically important jobs. How else could an industry that employs only around 40,000 of the 11.8 million employed people in Australia be seen as the backbone of the economy?[13]

While it's true that the 40,000 people who work in coal mining seems large when compared with the 8000 people who work in coal-fired power stations, coal mining is a tiny employer nationally. The manufacturing sector employs 870,000 people, while education employs 960,000. Health is the largest single sector, employing 1.52 million.[14]

According to the Queensland Resource Council, the mining industry as a whole was responsible for the employment of 366,000 people full-time in 2014–15. According to the Australian Bureau of Statistics, the number is 68,500.[15] One of them must be wrong. Either the public is being lied to by the boosters for the mining industry, or the public is being lied to by the ABS.

A former head of the Minerals Council of Australia, Mitch Hooke, told the million-strong audience of the ABC's *Q&A* program in July 2013 that mining was the biggest employer of Indigenous Australians.[16] He meant to say tenth-biggest. Health employs far more Indigenous Australians than mining, but econobabble, backed up by dodgy statistics, rarely goes unchallenged when spouted by a man wearing an expensive suit.

I know, I know, mining might be a small 'direct employer', but it creates lots of 'indirect jobs' (econobabble alert!) via 'the multiplier effect'. That's how the Queensland Minerals Council justifies its claim that mining employs seven times as many people as the ABS estimate. We'll look at the use of dodgy economic modelling in a subsequent chapter, but for now consider this. Building a hospital creates 'indirect jobs' in the construction industry, just like building a mine does. And most nurses spend their wages in the 'local economy', just like most miners. It's obvious when you stop and think about it, but employment in every industry creates 'indirect jobs'.

The coal industry employs less than 1 per cent of Australians (0.39 per cent, to be precise[17]), which means that more than 99 per cent of Australians don't work in coal mining. The so-called indirect jobs associated with mining are proportionate to the total employment, which means that mining, at best, creates 1 per cent of the 'indirect jobs' in Australia. But hats off to the mining companies: they have spent more money paying economists to exaggerate the size of their industry than any other industry.

Any structural change in the economy costs jobs, and any unexpected job loss is traumatic for those concerned. But the vast majority of people losing jobs in Australia today are not losing them because of climate policy. Steam-powered ships destroyed jobs in sailmaking, diesel trains destroyed jobs in the stream train business, and banning whaling had a devastating impact on employment in whaling. Good economic policy doesn't prevent desirable change; it invests in retraining and supporting people. Good social policy gives the unexpectedly unemployed a sense of security and support. It provides them with dignity.

The conservative governments and employer groups that have argued against policies that aim to reduce climate change have done nothing to improve the lot of the unemployed in Australia. In fact, both groups have worked hard to shed tens of thousands of workers from the public sector while arguing it should be harder to get unemployment benefits.

2. We can't afford schools and hospitals without all the tax paid by the mining industry.

> '*We are in the coal business. If you want decent hospitals,*
> *schools and police on the beat, we all need to understand that.*'
> — CAMPBELL NEWMAN,
>   FORMER QUEENSLAND PREMIER[18]

The taxes and royalties paid by all mining companies to all levels of government account for less than 5 per cent of government revenue.[19] And that's the total amount paid, not the net amount after we deduct the subsidies they receive. The Queensland government earns more from speeding fines and car registrations than it does from the coal industry.

These numbers come from state and federal budget papers. There is no 'modelling' or 'interpretation'. Thanks to data released by the ATO, the fact that the mining companies don't pay much tax, and some pay none, is clear for all to see. But a flood of econobabble, and much outright deception, has been effective in concealing this simple truth.

The vast majority of tax revenue collected in Australia comes from the income tax paid by workers, the GST paid by all citizens, and the corporate profit taxes paid by company shareholders. Mining is the backbone of neither our budgets nor our labour market. Indeed, according to the Queensland and West Australian Treasuries, it is a leech that is sucking us dry.

When pushed to defend the incredible cost to the taxpayer of building their ports, roads and rail lines, the mining industry falls back on claims about 'all the tax' mining companies pay. Leaving aside the fact that, as a proportion of state budgets, the mining industry simply doesn't pay a lot of tax, when taxpayers subsidise the mining industry another problem arises. A big one. The kind of problem that only econobabble can hide. This is what is known as 'opportunity cost'.

One of the first lessons taught in any economics class relates to the foundational economic principle of opportunity cost. Put simply, when a resource is scarce, then whenever that resource is dedicated to one pursuit, the 'opportunity' to use it for something else is lost. For example: your time is finite, and the time you spend reading this book is time you can't spend reading the Queensland budget papers.

Money is another scarce resource for state governments. And so when Queenslanders spend billions of dollars to pay for mining infrastructure, the opportunity to spend that money on hospitals and schools is lost. The same tax dollars can't fund both sectors at the same time.

The Queensland and West Australian Treasuries are adamant that a lot of taxpayer money is spent building infrastructure for the mining industry. The Queensland, West Australian and Commonwealth budget papers make clear that the mining industry doesn't pay a lot of tax. There is simply no truth to the assertion that the mining industry is what pays for our schools and hospitals. None. In fact, the opposite is the case. As the Queensland Treasury itself makes clear, our schools and hospitals are paying a high price for all of the subsidies given to the mining industry.

Such daylight robbery can only occur behind the cloak of econobabble.

3. A carbon tax would destroy our exports and ruin our economy

> 'The carbon tax will act as a wrecking ball across
> the economy.'
> — TONY ABBOTT [20]

While it is true that mining accounts for 48 per cent of Australia's exports, and that coal mining accounts for 12 per cent,[21] it's not at all clear whether that is a blessing or a curse. As the mining boom gathered pace from 2004, the value of mining exports increased from $42 billion to $154 billion in 2015.[22] The surge in exports saw Australia's exchange rate with the US dollar soar from US$0.80 to US$1.10. Imported cars became much cheaper, overseas holidays became much cheaper, and many middle-class people decided it was cheaper to get married in Bali or Fiji than in Australia.

Yet at the same time, the manufacturing industry suffered a significant decline, as did the tourism industry. The number of international tourists visiting Far North

Queensland plummeted from 865,000 in 2005–06 to 614,000 in 2011–12.[23] Foreign students switched from expensive Australian universities to 'cheaper options' in the United Kingdom and the United States. Agricultural producers had to accept much lower prices for their exports because of the high exchange rate.

So were all those extra mining exports good or bad? The answer, of course, depends on whether you were the Swiss owners of mining giant Glencore, or the Australian owner of a hotel in Cairns. Interestingly, while mining exports grew significantly during the mining boom (no surprise there), the level of exports in Australia as a whole didn't rise significantly as a percentage of GDP. Put simply, the mining exports cannibalised the non-mining exports. Economists use the more polite term *crowding out* to describe this effect.

All the export data described above is freely available to any politician, journalist or citizen who is willing to go the ABS website. Needless to say, few have taken up the opportunity.

Intriguingly, as the high exchange rate was devastating parts of the tourism and agriculture industries, their peak bodies were adamant that the opposite was true.[24] Despite the fact that overseas visitors to the Great Barrier Reef collapsed, and unemployment rates in Cairns hit 9.2 per cent, the peak tourism body seemed unconcerned that the high exchange rate was harming the industry. Bizarrely, however, as the exchange rate has fallen back towards its long-term average, the tourism industry argues that the declining exchange rate is giving it quite a boost![25]

Like so many politicians and journalists, it seems that even the industries that have been directly harmed by the mining boom are either confused by the econobabble or, worse, willing to use econobabble to conceal the need to confront big industries such as mining.

So much for exports – but will a carbon tax destroy the economy?

The people who ran the campaign against the carbon tax are the same people who argue that personal income tax wrecks the economy, that company tax wrecks the economy and, yep, that tax generally wrecks the economy. While there is no doubt that there were mistakes in the way the carbon price was designed and sold to the public, there is also no doubt that the carbon tax package came with very big personal income tax cuts.

Virtually every trained economist would agree with the statement that it is more economically efficient to collect tax revenue from products you are trying to discourage (alcohol, tobacco, emissions) than something you are trying to encourage (fresh food, books, work). The fact that the carbon tax debate was lost on economic grounds is the most exquisite demonstration of the power of econobabble.

(It's fun to note, by the way, that the party which introduced the GST also won the public debate about the carbon tax on the basis that it was 'a great big new tax on everything'. Well played!)

From the time that the carbon price was proposed at the 2007 election to the time it was legislated in 2011, the Australian exchange rate surged from below US\$0.70 in 2008 to US\$1.10 in 2011 before plunging back to US\$0.75 in 2015. The idea that a modest carbon price rather than the impact of the mining boom would 'destroy the competitiveness' of Australian exporters is simply absurd. But then again, so was the fact that Australia faced a 'budget emergency'.

Rising electricity prices played an important role in destroying popular support for the carbon price, but in fact these had almost nothing to do with the carbon price. The carbon price did increase the average electricity bill by \$172 – for which most houses received significant compensation – but the cost of 'distribution services' (commonly known as the 'poles and wires') pushed the average bill up by \$580 between 2008 and 2014.[26] This, plus the costs of managing customers, advertising and paying profits to the owners of the electricity companies, was what was driving up electricity prices, but the carbon price took the blame. It was the scapegoat that distracted an entire nation from the truth.

Tony Abbott went to the 2013 election thundering about the 'budget emergency' and promising to 'axe the carbon tax'. What he didn't say was that while he was planning to scrap the carbon tax, he was also planning to keep the expensive tax cuts that had come with it. He was also happy for the companies that were paid billions of dollars in compensation for the carbon tax to hang on to the taxpayers' money, even though he was abolishing the thing they were being compensated for. Budget emergency? Not so much.

CONCLUSION

The coal mining industry and coal-fired electricity generators are not big employers. They don't pay a lot of tax, but they do get a lot of subsidies.

There are lots of reasons to tackle climate change, only a handful of which are economic. As a society, we are usually willing to pay a small amount now to protect ourselves against future risk. We call it insurance. Few people, having spent a thousand dollars insuring their house against the unlikely risk of fire, feel they have 'wasted their money' when it doesn't burn down.

Even if tackling climate change was somehow bad for the economy, it would still be a good idea to avoid it. But in fact doing something about climate change is a bargain.

For reasons beyond the scope of this chapter, we have been trained to think about responding to climate change differently to how we respond to other structural changes. While people talk endlessly about the 'costs' of tackling climate change, who remembers hearing people talk about the costs of switching from video recorders to DVD players, or the costs of switching from film cameras to digital cameras? Let's be clear: those transitions resulted in hundreds of thousands of job losses. Businesses went broke (remember Kodak?) and 'mum and dad investors' lost money.

The economy is changing all the time. People lose and gain jobs all the time. Except when it comes to climate change, the business community and the so-called free-market economists applaud such change. Have you ever heard a business lobby argue that emails were destroying the postal industry, and that we should therefore oppose the use of email?

Carbon pricing is good policy, but there is no economic or political necessity to win the fight about carbon pricing first. Scrapping subsidies, opposing new coal mines on prime farmland, encouraging energy efficiency and subsidising renewable energy (at least until the coal subsidies are removed) provide easy, effective and politically popular ways to rapidly reduce greenhouse gas emissions.

While collecting more tax from pollution and less from other sources is a good long-term goal, it will be politically easier once the coal mining subsidies have been scrapped and the renewable energy industry has had more time to grow. Winning the political argument about climate change will never be easy. But it should be impossible to lose the economic argument about it.

CHAPTER 3
WHAT REALLY CAUSES UNEMPLOYMENT?

When it comes to unemployment, it is far easier to blame the victim than it is to solve the problem. And victim blaming remains the first instinct among many conservative politicians and 'economic commentators'. In his 2014 budget speech, then treasurer Joe Hockey announced his plan to make it harder for young unemployed people to access financial support, so that they would not 'embark on a life on welfare'. Under Hockey's 'plan' to tackle unemployment, those under thirty would have to wait up to six months before the government would give them any aid.[1]

But what do these same politicians say when older Australians are unemployed? The political and economic power of baby boomers makes it harder for conservatives to point to perceived moral failings to explain their job-lessness. So unemployment among older Australians is usually put down to discrimination. In the same budget speech, Hockey declared:

> For Australians over 50, we also want to give you every opportunity to participate in the workforce. But I know how hard it can be for older Australians to find a job.
>
> There needs to be a change in the culture of many businesses towards older workers.
>
> We will help change that culture by providing a payment of up to $10,000 to a business that employs an Australian over the age of 50 who has been on unemployment benefits or the Disability Support Pension for six months.[2]

While the young and inexperienced are wholly responsible for their own destiny and undeserving of government help, those over fifty are victims of a culture of discrimination that requires taxpayer money to fix.

Some employers likely do discriminate against older workers when recruiting for some roles. But when you take into account the discrimination experienced by Aboriginal Australians, people from a non-English speaking background, single mothers, young people and people with disabilities, the notion that older Australians are the group that suffers the most discrimination, and therefore are in need of special funding, is as ridiculous as it is politically convenient.

As will be explained below, successive governments have considered some level of unemployment not just inevitable but economically desirable. The question for governments, then, is not 'How do we solve unemployment?' but 'How do we use unemployment for our political advantage?' Unfortunately, blaming the victim is an easy way for governments to sidestep the need to solve the problem, while also signalling to the majority of voters who do have jobs that the government is on 'their' side. And siding with the majority is usually a good idea in a democracy.

LABOUR MARKETS DON'T WORK THE WAY BUSINESS LEADERS SAY THEY DO

Most of what you have been told about how labour markets work is the kind of rubbish that would see you fail a first-year economics course. But that is hardly surprising, given that most of the people talking about wages and unemployment have no training in economics. While they may lack qualifications, they rarely lack confidence. And they certainly don't see a need to be consistent in their arguments. Consider the following:

- When the economy is growing rapidly, employer groups typically say it is a bad time to raise wages, as that would cause inflation. And when the economy is growing slowly, employer groups typically say it is also a bad time to raise wages, as that would cause more unemployment. So when would it be a good time to raise wages?

- We are always told that investors 'need certainty' in order to make long-term decisions, but that workers 'need to be flexible'. Why do we expect young people with no money to borrow tens of thousands of dollars to fund their degrees, with no certainty that their skills will be valuable in a decade's time, yet we accept that billionaires with diversified investment portfolios can't make a new investment unless governments promise them 'certainty'?

- Why do wage rises cause inflation or unemployment, but profit rises provide evidence that the economy is doing well?

- If the wealthiest and most productive economies in the world have high minimum wages, why would we as a nation pursue a lower minimum wage?

Economists call our workplaces the 'labour market', and the vast majority of trained economists would agree that it is one of the most complicated and hard-to-predict markets that exist. The reason it's so hard to analyse is that people are much less uniform than most other things economists study. Workers are different to each other, managers are different to each other, companies are different to each other, cultures are different to each other – and all of those differences keep changing. If economists' simplistic model of 'perfect competition' struggles to explain the market for orange juice or coffee, what chance does it have in the labour market?

But despite the widespread acceptance among trained economists that 'labour markets are different', conservative politicians and self-appointed 'business leaders' typically rely on arguments and analogies based on 'common sense' ideas about what causes unemployment – and they're almost always wrong.

IF THERE WAS A SIMPLE SOLUTION TO UNEMPLOYMENT, WOULDN'T SOMEONE HAVE FOUND IT BY NOW?

Populist economic prescriptions are like fad diets. Don't eat meat. Don't eat fat. Don't eat carbs. Only eat meat. Fat is good but sugar is evil … The problem faced by real nutritionists is that there is no such thing as a 'super food' or 'slimming secret', and it's hard to sell books that don't promise something new.

People's metabolisms, like their prospects in the labour market, are all different. But no one ever lost weight while taking in more energy than they use up. And no government ever solved unemployment by training more workers than there are jobs available.

After hundreds of years in hundreds of countries, there is no agreed and foolproof solution to unemployment. While there is some agreement among economists about what does and doesn't work in the short term, there is very little agreement about what the 'best thing' to do about unemployment is. What we have instead are the equivalent of fad diets.

Consider the following 'fads' among the commentariat:

- In the 1980s, the Japanese economy was held up as the one we should emulate. Their rigid employment practices, the way they offered jobs for life to 'company men', and even their early-morning calisthenics were, we were told at the time, the reason for the Japanese economic miracle.

- In the 1990s we were supposed to emulate the United States. Its 'flexible' labour market, low wages, lack of sick pay and holiday pay, and the way its service sector worked for tips, were, we were told, the reasons for the US economic miracle.

- The 'Asian Tiger' economies – of Hong Kong, Singapore, South Korea and Taiwan – briefly provided another model for us to emulate in the 1990s. They provided a combination of the US-style lack of basic protections for workers with much lower rates of tax than either the United States or Japan.

- The 'Celtic Tiger' economy of Ireland in the early
  2000s briefly provided 'proof' that low taxes, especially
  for corporations, were the key to low unemployment.
  You don't hear much about copying Ireland since the
  global financial crisis of 2007–08.

The problem for the econobabblers in Australia is that our
response to the GFC – a government-funded economic
stimulus package worth around $100 billion – was held
up as a success story by other countries as a way of saving
jobs and staving off recession. Unfortunately for the job-
less in Australia, however, unemployment in recent years
has started to rise again.

Just as Australians were once encouraged to look to
Asia to learn what 'good economic policy' looked like,
these days sensible Europeans are asking how Australia
did it. While it was mainly greeted with chuckles in Australia, the fact that Wayne Swan was declared finance
minister of the year in 2011 was clear evidence that the
world thought we were doing something right.

In the lead-up to the 2013 federal election, the Nobel
Prize–winning economist Joseph Stiglitz was visiting
Australia. He observed:

> For an American, Australia's anxiety about deficit and
> debt is a little amusing. Australia's budget deficit is less
> than half that of the US and its net debt is less than an
> eighth of the country's gross domestic product.

Most countries would envy Australia's economy. During the global recession, Kevin Rudd's government implemented one of the strongest Keynesian stimulus packages in the world. That package was delivered early, with cash grants that could be spent quickly followed by longer-term investments that buoyed confidence and activity over time. In many other countries, stimulus was too small and arrived too late, after jobs and confidence were already lost.

In Australia the stimulus helped avoid a recession and saved up to 200,000 jobs. And new research shows that stimulus may have also actually reduced government debt over time. Evidence from the crisis suggests that, when the economy is weak, the long-run tax revenue benefits of keeping businesses afloat and people in work can be greater than the short-run expenditure on stimulus measures. That means that a well-targeted fiscal stimulus might actually reduce public debt in the long run.[3]

Tony Abbott, a man with no training in economics but a belief that 'sound economic management is in [his party's] DNA',[4] disagreed with the Labor government's approach.

Either Stiglitz or Abbott was utterly wrong.

THE FALLACY OF COMPOSITION

One of the reasons labour market economics is so difficult to understand is the blurry line between why some
individuals earn more than others (a microeconomic
problem) and why average wages across the whole economy are rising faster or slower than average (a macro-
economic problem). While microeconomics can help
explain why some people are unemployed at the moment
(they likely have lower levels of skills and experience
than the employed), it can tell us nothing about why the
ranks of the unemployed swelled by hundreds of thousands in the early 1990s. (Hint: it wasn't an outbreak of
unskilfulness.)

Economics isn't unique when it comes to inconsist-
ency between accepted theories. Physicists, for example,
accept that the 'laws of physics' which help explain how
cannonballs move through the air have no predictive
power when trying to explain how electrons move around.
While physicists dream of developing a 'grand unified
theory of everything', they accept that, for the time being,
they need different models to explain big things and little
things. They also accept that their model of big things
and their model of little things are contradictory at times,
and that, in some sense, both their models must be a
bit wrong.

While most trained economists accept that our microeconomic model explaining why a particular individual
is unemployed does nothing to explain the national

unemployment rate, politicians and business leaders often ignore this simple truth. Their denial (or failure to understand) means that they can blame the unemployed for their joblessness, but it does nothing to help them solve the actual problem of mass unemployment.

Common sense says that what works for an individual should work for anyone else who tries it. Economists know that we can't make that assumption – it's simply incorrect. Indeed, it's an error made so commonly that we have a name for it: the 'fallacy of composition'.

Let's consider an example. If you steal biscuits or toilet paper from your workplace, you'll probably save yourself a bit of money on biscuits and toilet paper. But if you tell everyone at your work about your idea and everyone starts doing it, then your employers will probably install a vending machine for snacks instead, and one of those annoying toilet paper dispensers that only gives you one small piece of paper at a time. What works when one person does it doesn't work when everyone does it.

The same is true with car parking. Imagine your friends are complaining that they can never find a car park near the cafe you meet at, so you tell them where your 'secret parking spot' is. Do you think that the next time you and your friends arrange to go to the cafe, you will all find the same convenient secret park? What is true for the individual doesn't always hold true for the collective.

This is especially so for the labour market. If you were having trouble getting a job and I offered to call some friends and tell them what a great employee you were, I could probably get you a job – but I can't do that for lots of other people at the same time. You guessed it: what works for an individual doesn't work for a large group.

Remarkably, Joe Hockey as treasurer didn't seem to understand the fallacy of composition. Consider his response to concerns about housing affordability in Sydney. 'The starting point for a first home buyer is to get a good job that pays good money,' he said. 'If you've got a good job and it pays good money and you have security in relation to that job, then you can go to the bank and you can borrow money and that's readily affordable.'[5]

Mr Hockey was pilloried by his opponents for the insensitivity of his comment, but the fundamentally flawed logic of his advice went largely unremarked. At a competitive house auction, the market price will be determined by the bidders' willingness and ability to pay. Having a big deposit, a high income or generous parents will all help an individual 'win' at such an auction. But we can't all have better jobs than each other.

Nor can we all be better trained than everyone else. Surges in unemployment are not evidence of a 'loss of skills', or of an 'outbreak of laziness'. They are evidence of a shortage of jobs relative to the number of job seekers. Helping people to have better interview skills might change who gets a job, but it can't possibly affect how many people get a job.

Just as household analogies of budgets don't work very well for governments, individual stories about how to get a job aren't very useful for understanding how labour markets work. Everyone knows someone who is too lazy to apply for a job – and every conservative politician seems to know someone who applied for a hundred jobs before getting a job as a cleaner, and then went on to rise through the ranks of the company. Even if such stories are true, they are irrelevant when it comes to explaining why unemployment grew by 6.5 million people in the United States after the GFC. Does anyone really think those 6.5 million people suddenly became lazy?

BLAMING THE INERT BLUDGER

Anyone suggesting that a simple fix for unemployment would be to fix all of the unemployed people is either lying to themselves about how much economics they understand, or lying to the public about how much economics they understand.

Politicians and businesspeople who think that their own personal story – or, worse, some story they heard about someone else – qualifies them to participate in a public debate about how to tackle unemployment should be laughed off the stage. What follows are three more of the most common but wrong-headed opinions about the employment market in Australia.

1. Unemployment is caused by bludgers who won't look for work or take the jobs on offer.

> *'I think there is a risk of people getting too fussy, people becoming job snobs. That's to say, yes they want to work, but only on their own terms.'*
> —TONY ABBOTT AS EMPLOYMENT MINISTER IN
>   1999[6]

While this view is common among the conservative commentariat, it is a pretty harsh assessment of the country folk who typically vote for the National Party. Average unemployment rates are usually much higher in the bush than they are in the cities, so if the conservatives are right that unemployment is caused by the laziness or 'job-snobbishness' of the unemployed, then it would seem that growing up in the country has a terrible impact on work ethic. Of course, it's possible that there simply aren't enough jobs in rural areas for the people who live there.

2. The unemployed should move to find work.

> *'If people choose to live where there's no jobs, obviously it's very, very difficult to close the gap.'*
> —TONY ABBOTT IN 2015, ON THE 'LIFESTYLE
>   CHOICES' OF INDIGENOUS AUSTRALIANS[7]

Have you ever noticed that the same conservatives who put so much emphasis on 'family values' are quick to encourage the unemployed to leave their families behind? And while they say Indigenous people should leave their ancestral lands behind in order to find work, they nevertheless insist that public money should be spent to keep farmers on land they have farmed 'for generations'.

The fact that most people need to live near their workplace is a major reason that 'labour markets' are harder to explain, and to fix, than markets for commodities such as fruit or computers. The 'social' and 'personal' reasons that people want or need to live in a particular place are significant. A large number of Australians have significant roles caring for their elderly parents, and many others rely on support from their extended families. The idea that they should abandon such support and move, which in turn would create greater demand on publicly provided care services, is surely inconsistent with the idea of 'looking after your own' typically championed by conservatives.

3. The unemployed lack the skills employers require.

The strangest way to blame the unemployed is to finger them for lacking the experience that getting a job would give them. It's like blaming a starving person for not eating enough.

Imagine the following. There are two applicants for a job in a shop. One applicant has twelve months' experience and has completed a one-month course in retail management. The other has neither experience nor training. If all other things were equal (an economist's favourite assumption), who do you think would get the job?

But the politically convenient idea that unemployment in general is caused by a 'lack of skills' is economically flawed. The lack of trained mobile phone engineers didn't impede the rapid growth of the mobile phone industry, and the abundance of trained photograph development technicians did nothing to stop the collapse of the photographic film industry and the rise of digital cameras. Growing industries train the staff they need in order to keep growing.

Imagine that we wanted to 'fix' unemployment in a small country town of 1500 people, and we now 'know' that those with training and experience are more likely to get jobs than those without. In our small town there are thirty unemployed young people. Rather than let them 'waste their lives' on unemployment benefits, the government implements an 'earn or learn' policy and requires all of the town's unemployed people to do a course in retail management, and to do associated unpaid 'work experience'. Do you think that all thirty will be employed in a retail venture at the end of the course? In fact, do you think more or fewer people will be employed in the town's shops, since the young people are required to work in them for free? In what world does the number of trained retail workers determine the demand for products in a shop?

Employers don't employ people simply because they have skills, but because there is enough demand to justify employing people to provide the goods or services consumers want. Increasing the number of trained retail workers will no more increase the number of people employed in retail than increasing the number of car tyres produced would increase the number of cars sold.

Of course, well-targeted investment in education and training can be good for individuals, and for the whole economy. There is great evidence that suggests that such investment drives productivity growth and economic growth, and helps individuals to enjoy their work more. But it is a fallacy of composition to suggest that because we train people, jobs will be created for them. They won't, and to say otherwise is a cruel exercise in blaming the victim.

WAGES ARE TOO HIGH!

'Our merchants and masters complain much of the bad effects of high wages in raising the price and lessening the sale of goods. They say nothing concerning the bad effects of high profits. They are silent with regard to the pernicious effects of their own gains. They complain only of those of other people.'

—ADAM SMITH, THE WEALTH OF NATIONS

Every conservative knows that high wages cause unemployment. One of the many problems with this belief is that rising wages and rapid job growth usually go hand-in-hand. And the fact that real wages have fallen in the

United States while unemployment has risen. And the fact that Sydney and outback New South Wales have the same award wages but vastly different unemployment rates.

As discussed above, the labour market is far more complicated than the markets for razor blades or orange juice. There is no clear evidence that increasing the minimum wage increases unemployment. Indeed, numerous US studies have shown that lowering the (state-determined) minimum wage often leads to increased unemployment.

One of the biggest problems in this 'debate' is that conservative commentators typically talk about 'common sense', and ask lots of businesspeople for their 'expert advice'. In reality, many of the businesspeople who are asked this question have a large and obvious conflict of interest: they prefer to pay lower wages, so they can make larger profits. (And, for the conservatives, the only thing that works better than blaming unemployment on the greed of low-paid workers is blaming the unions that represent them.)

It takes effort and skill to run a business well, but it doesn't take an understanding of economics. The fact that businesspeople believe that reducing wages will lead to a reduction in unemployment is about as relevant as young people believing its okay to text and drive because they have good reflexes. Self-belief and self-interest can be a heady brew, but listening to those who drink too heavily from it can have devastating consequences.

As we've seen, so-called 'common sense' about training

unemployed workers easily leads people astray in debates about the labour market, and the same is true of 'common sense' about wages. While it is true that rising wages can lead to fewer jobs, it is also true that falling wages can lead to fewer jobs. Wages are not simply a 'cost to business' – they are the major source of income in Australia, and in turn play a major role in determining the demand for everything, from clothes and food to cars and holidays, and so for labour.

While cutting the wages of an individual working for a small business might lead to an extra shift being offered to someone else (or not), slowing the rate of wages growth across the economy might lead to whole retail chains shutting down.

This is probably the perfect time to start talking about macroeconomics.

DO PEOPLE WHO GET PAY CUTS SPEND MORE OR LESS MONEY IN THE LOCAL SHOPS?

The next time you hear someone talking about the need to cut wages in order to boost employment, just ask them this: 'What will happen to consumer spending if we cut people's wages?'

The problem for the average conservative is that simple stories with lots of reference to 'common sense' are their stock in trade. And while common sense allegedly tells us that high wages cause unemployment, common sense also tells us that lower wages will reduce the amount of money that people will spend in shops. At this point, the econobabble usually goes up a notch as the 'expert' tries to shift the debate back to the personal failings of the unemployed.

The reason it is hard to answer the question is because it is a really hard question. Indeed, it's the kind of question that economists have been arguing about for centuries. The root of the problem is that wages are both a cost to business and the major source of income in the economy. It's easy enough to ignore the overall impact of lowering one person's wage at one small business. It is ridiculous, though, to ignore the overall impact of lowering the wages of millions of people.

But this is exactly what most conservatives do when they trot out their folksy anecdotes about the economy and how the greed of the poor is what causes unemployment. Remember, actual economics is a lot more complicated, subtle and contestable than the econobabble of shock-jocks and tabloid politicians.

Imagine a small town with 1500 people, three pubs and a high rate of unemployment. Let's suppose that one of the publicans uses some 'common sense' to talk the government into an experiment, in the hope of increasing employment. Having received the nod from the government, the town's 'top pub' is allowed to halve the wages of its bar staff. All of a sudden, the publican finds that her business is much more 'competitive', and she reduces her food and beer prices to attract more customers.

It works, and before she knows it she is putting on more staff to cope with all her new customers.

After she reports her success to the government, the experiment is expanded and the other two pubs are allowed to slash their wages too. They quickly cut their prices to win their customers back. I'm sure you can see where this is heading. Things start to slow down at the top pub as their new customers drift back to the other two.

The fallacy of composition has reared its common sense–destroying head again. What was true for one pub doesn't hold true for all pubs. In fact, it's possible that the general cut in wages might lead to an overall reduction in beer and food sales, and ultimately a reduction in the number of staff employed.

Workers are customers as well, and this means that wages are not just a cost to business but also an injection of demand into the economy.

When a pub halves the wages of its staff, they probably won't spend as much on beer and grub themselves. Most businesspeople see their job (and their skill) as gaining an advantage over their competitors, and when they think about the opportunity of paying their workers less, they aren't thinking about the fact that their competitors will be able to do the same. Unfortunately, most businesspeople don't think as big as Henry Ford, who realised earlier than most that his workers were also his customers.

Evidence doesn't change the minds of most conservatives, but evidence and arguments can change the minds of the people they are talking to. Economists have spent hundreds of years arguing with each other about what causes unemployment, so it's unlikely that you will land a killer blow in any debate you have with a conservative. But you don't need to land a killer blow to win a debate; often you just need to make your opponent seem foolish and belligerent. Given the refusal of many conservatives to admit that training can't create jobs, and that economy-wide wage cuts can lead to job cuts, it's usually not hard to make them appear both.

And remember: the more econobabble they speak, the simpler you should make your follow-up question. The average observer can spot a bullshitter when they see one.

THE UGLY TRUTH

Okay, it's time to break the big news. Governments in Australia like to have at least half a million unemployed people at any point in time. It doesn't matter how skilled they are, or what the wage rate is. Successive governments in Australia have, for decades, sought to 'manage the economy' in such a way that the unemployment rate hovers around 5 per cent.

If unemployment falls 'too fast' and the unemployment rate gets 'too low', Treasury (the folk who advise governments on spending and taxing policy) and the Reserve Bank (the folk who set official interest rates) get nervous. They're afraid that the economy might become 'overheated' and cause inflation – and they fear inflation more than they dislike unemployment. So when the economy is growing fast and unemployment is falling, the Treasury and the RBA use the budget (fiscal policy) or interest rates (monetary policy) to put 'downward pressure on demand'. That's a polite way of saying 'create a bit more unemployment'.

You don't believe me? Here's the RBA describing how monetary policy works: 'Substantial rises in interest rates, designed to restrain inflationary booms, have been followed by contractions in demand and a reduction in inflation. Conversely, substantial interest rate reductions have been followed by periods of significantly faster growth.' When translated, this means that lifting interest rates slows the economy down, and lowering interest rates speeds it up – and rapidly growing economies create more jobs than slowly growing economies.

The problem for unemployed people is that the RBA usually starts to get 'nervous' about inflation whenever the unemployment rate gets below 5 per cent. Put another way, if there are fewer than 500,000 unemployed people in Australia, the RBA is likely to start trying to slow the economy down, in order to make sure inflation doesn't grow. This is good news for people who worry about inflation, and bad news for the 600,000 people who can't find jobs.

Why on earth would they do this, I hear you ask. It's a surprisingly simple question that is rarely put to treasurers and prime ministers. The best answer I can give you is that they fear that if they don't maintain a large pool of unemployed people, workers might be confident enough to demand higher wages; and employers, in turn, would increase the prices they charge for their products in order to cover the resulting higher wages. This is called a 'wage–price spiral', but with Australian firms facing stiff competition from imports, it's hard to see how they could simply pass on price rises in this way.

I wish I could give you a better answer, and I encourage you to ask others to explain it. After thirty years of asking, I'm yet to hear an answer I find persuasive.

Mentioning Marx isn't the best way to win an economic debate in Australia, but it's interesting to note that he, too, talked about employers' desire for a 'reserve army of labour' that would – you guessed it – keep 'downward pressure' on wages.[8]

SO IF WE CAN'T REDUCE UNEMPLOYMENT, WHAT CAN WE DO?

We could reduce unemployment if we wanted to. But successive governments have accepted the advice of Treasury and the RBA that to reduce unemployment below their estimate of its 'natural rate' (or Non-Accelerating Inflation Rate of Unemployment – NAIRU to its friends) of around 5 per cent will cause inflation.

So, if we accept this premise (as prime ministers Howard, Rudd, Gillard, Abbott and Turnbull have) and agree that we can't – or won't – reduce unemployment to anything like zero, what can we do? The main thing we can do is to increase the productivity of labour, and be nice to the people who are unemployed, as they are keeping inflation low for the rest of us.

Virtually all economists would agree that investment in general education and specific training are good ways to create more productive workers. And while productivity growth can be disruptive for those who, like the New South Wales miners, lose their jobs to machines, in the long run most people would prefer to live in a high-productivity (and high-wage) country such as Australia than in a low-productivity (and low-wage) country such as Bangladesh.

As discussed in Chapter 8, it is interesting to note that the conservative politicians who claim that they want to increase economic growth systematically refuse to invest more taxpayers' money in the thing that nearly all economists agree would boost economic growth in the long run: education for all.

CONCLUSION

Econobabble is used to conceal the horrible truth about unemployment from the masses, and to blame unemployment on the victims of government policy. Ruthless, huh?

While most right-wing shock-jocks 'know' that higher wages cause higher inflation and higher unemployment, they probably have no idea that successive governments have deliberately sought to maintain half a million or so unemployed people in order to keep wages and inflation from growing 'too fast'. The unemployed play an essential role in our economy. They keep inflation down for the rest of us. But rather than thank them, we usually demean them. We blame unemployment not on the RBA's interest-rate policy but on the unemployed masses' lack of motivation and experience. Except, of course, for baby boomers, who, we are told, suffer from the most extreme form of labour market discrimination.

Conservatives tell fairy-tales about the handful of unemployed people who work their way to the top in order to hide the truth: that policy-makers target a minimum level of unemployment and use the budget and interest rates to ensure that we never have a 'shortage' of unemployed people. Of course, most conservative commentators have no idea what the RBA really means when it says the labour market risks becoming 'overheated'. The next time they tell you it's common sense that high wages cause unemployment, just ask them what they think the natural rate of unemployment is. If they don't know, you win. And if they do know, you win.

Unemployment isn't caused by 'job snobs'. It's caused by snobs who hate it when the economy starts creating 'too many jobs'.

CHAPTER 4
DEBT, DEFICITS
AND BUDGET HONESTY

E ach year the US president spells out their accomplishments and their vision in the State of the Union address. Each year in Australia, the federal treasurer spells out the state of our finances and the government's latest savings measures in the Commonwealth budget speech. It says something about us that our politicians seem to be more worried about money than the Americans.

More econobabble is spoken about budget deficits and public-sector debt than about any other issue. Newspapers once reported on budgets with headlines like 'Beer and cigs up'. These days, there are sixteen-page budget supplements telling us about 'outyears' and 'forwards', and attempting to decode the kind of accounting trickery that now dominates the budget papers (and once led to the collapse of Enron).

Don't get me wrong – budgets do matter. How a government plans to collect taxes and spend money has a significant impact on individuals, communities, industries and the economy as a whole. But the way that budget has become a talisman that proves the superior morality of one side of parliament, rather than a fat report that shows how spending priorities have changed in the past twelve months, has done nothing to improve the quality of economic (or political) debate in Australia.

Like all econobabble, most of the debate around the budget is designed to conceal, not reveal. Australia is one of the wealthiest countries in the world, and we live at the wealthiest point in world history. Australians can afford to do anything we want, but we can't afford to do everything we want. If we want to continue to be one of the lowest-taxing countries in the world, then we won't be able to spend as much on schools, hospitals and transport as northern European countries do. And if we want to lower our tax collections even further, to emulate those of our South Pacific neighbours, then we will ultimately have to lower our health and education spending as well.

Budgets do not document the morality of a government, but they do document its recent performance and its planned priorities. But over the past two decades the debate has shifted. We once asked: 'Do we want to spend more money on the services we value?', but now it is simply: 'Is the budget in surplus or deficit?'

WE NEED TO TALK ABOUT THE WORD *SURPLUS*

The fact that a budget deficit seems 'bad' and a budget surplus seems 'good' is a trick of language, not a truth of economics. *Surplus* is a positive word. We never say people put on weight because of a surplus of food; we say they overeat. And we don't say someone died from a surplus of heroin; we call it an overdose. Language also tells us that a *deficit* is something we should avoid – think of a learning deficit or an attention-deficit disorder. But economics tells us no such thing about the relative merits of budget deficits and surpluses.

Simplistic analogies about managing household budgets do nothing to help us understand the role of government budgets in managing the macroeconomy. While the following pages will deal with the econobabble that dominates debates about our budget, we should first kill off the absurd notion that 'common sense' tells us that budget deficits are bad and surpluses are good.

In a speech entitled 'The Case for Change', Joe Hockey declared, 'to put it in the simplest terms, we are spending money we don't have'.[1] Putting complicated, multifaceted problems in their 'simplest terms' is often risky, but let's consider what would happen if anyone actually took the former Coalition treasurer's advice seriously:

- A responsible young person would never borrow money to fund their university degree (and a responsible government would never lend them that money).

- A responsible household would never borrow money to buy a house or a car.

- A responsible company would never borrow money to invest in a new factory.

- The Menzies government, which ran deficits for nine of its eighteen years in power, would have never borrowed money to build the Snowy Mountains Hydro-electric Scheme.

I know, I know, those 'deficits' are different because the people and companies that are 'spending like drunken sailors' and 'racking up debt' are actually making long-term investments. But did you know that the Commonwealth's budget deficit includes all of its capital spending on assets that will last for decades? And do you realise that spending Commonwealth money on education is specifically designed to increase Australia's gross domestic product in the future?

The idea that it is 'common sense' to never spend more than you earn makes absolutely no sense. It's not how people run their households, and it's not how business-people run their companies. For a government that can determine its own income (by varying taxes) and whose debts are written in a currency that it can issue, the notion is absolutely irrelevant.

COMPANIES DON'T ASPIRE TO RUN A BUDGET SURPLUS

'Households understand they must live within their means. Governments must do so too.'
—TONY SHEPHERD, CHAIR OF THE NATIONAL COMMISSION OF AUDIT, 2014[2]

At the peak of the mining boom, a period in which world commodity prices were higher than they had been in a century, BHP and Rio Tinto were running budget deficits. They were spending more than they were earning. They were, according to Joe Hockey and Tony Shepherd's home-spun wisdom, 'living beyond their means'.

BHP has been operating for 150 years and is still in debt. Its regular budget deficits mean that its debt has 'blown out' in recent years, but, presumably to Joe Hockey's amazement, the company's board members aren't worried about their 'profligacy'. Indeed, so unconcerned is the BHP board about the size of their budget deficit that it's never even mentioned in the company's annual report.

Read that again if you need to. Companies don't care about their 'budget deficit' or 'budget surplus'. They don't even talk about them. They do talk about their profits a lot, but a *profit* and a *surplus* are entirely unrelated concepts. Econobabblers suggest they are the same, but they are not calculated in the same way and they do not mean the same thing.

Just as our brains tell us that deficits are bad and surpluses are good, years of econobabble have trained most people to think of a budget surplus as the public-sector equivalent of a profit, and a budget deficit as a loss. But again, we must understand that a *deficit* and a *loss* are entirely different things. For centuries priests told us that the Earth was the centre of the universe – but just saying it for a long time doesn't make it true.

WHY *RUNNING A SURPLUS* IS NOTHING LIKE *MAKING A PROFIT*, AND WHY PEOPLE WHO SAY IT IS ARE EITHER IGNORANT OR LYING

A budget surplus exists when you receive more money in a given period than you expend in that period. When a surplus is distributed to its owners – such as when Kevin Rudd's government posted everyone a cheque for $900 during the GFC – that is treated as money going out, and so reduces the size of the surplus. Now, hold that thought.

A profit means that more money was received in a given period than was spent to produce it. Unlike a surplus, a profit does not treat the full cost of buying long-lived assets (such as a house, a factory or a piece of machinery) as an expense to be deducted from the revenue received in that period. Also unlike a surplus, if a company paid a dividend of $900 to each of its shareholders, that 'return of funds to owners' would not be treated as an expense, and so would not be deducted from the calculated profit of the firm.

Do these boring definitions and accounting differences matter? You bet they do. Let's look at an example.

According to the ABS, the total amount of money spent by all levels of Australian government on 'capital investment' in 2013–14 was $55.2 billion. And in the same year the total 'cash deficit' of all levels of government was $47.6 billion.[3] So what, I hear you yawn. Well, think of it this way.

The 'reckless governments' that are 'spending irresponsibly' and creating a 'burden' for future generations are actually spending an enormous amount of money today that will deliver benefits for future generations. Indeed, if you took all of the capital spending out of the budgets and treated it separately (as governments used to), then you would see that recurrent spending (which also includes spending on things that create future benefits, such as education) is actually less than recurrent revenue.

All of that 'unaffordable' welfare spending is, it seems, entirely affordable – even taking into consideration our desire to remain as one of the lowest-taxing nations in the developed world, and our agreement for high-income retirees not to pay a cent in tax on their multimillion-dollar retirement incomes, and our willingness to let multinational companies such as Apple and Google pay virtually no tax here.

Imagine what we could 'afford' to do if we chose to collect the OECD average rate of tax each year. In 2015–16 that would have meant an additional $100 billion to spend on extra services. That could fund quite a bit of investment in schools, roads and hospitals, with plenty left over to balance the budget, if that's what we wanted to do.

CONSERVATIVES LOVE BUDGET DEFICITS

In 2014 the Coalition government said we were 'living beyond our means' and faced a 'budget emergency', which, if not addressed, would lead us 'into the eye of an economic storm'.[4] Sound scary? Relax. Joe Hockey did.

In 2015 then treasurer Hockey announced that even though the deficit had grown, the storm had passed. Indeed, during his 2015 budget speech he was decidedly chipper. In twelve months he shifted from preaching doom and gloom to urging everyone to look on the bright side of life. He used his budget speech to tell Australians to 'have a go'.

After Tony Abbott was booted out by the Liberal backbench, the newly installed prime minister, Malcolm Turnbull, said that we needed to spend up big on infrastructure. But his new treasurer, Scott Morrison, simultaneously said the budget had a spending problem and that we needed to cut taxes.

What Joe Hockey's remarkable backflip and the fundamental contradiction between Turnbull and Morrison show is that the only thing conservatives hate more than budget deficits is collecting the taxes to fix them.

American conservatives have a name for their strategy of causing budget deficits in order to justify cutting services: 'starving the beast'. I call it the 'right-wing ratchet', and it works like this.

When the economy is booming, you cut taxes for the wealthy. You tell people it will be 'good for the economy', and that 'the markets will respond well'. A few years later, when the economy and tax revenue begin to falter, you cut spending on the poor. Introduce co-payments, tighten welfare eligibility criteria and, if you're feeling particularly brave, cut taxes for the wealthy again. Tell the punters that the tax cuts will 'give investors confidence', and that 'the markets will respond well'. Better yet, rebadge the tax cuts for high-income earners as 'investment incentives'. Everyone loves incentives.

When the economy is going well, deliver for the rich, and when the economy is going badly, you guessed it, deliver for the rich.

It's hard to believe that such a simple strategy could work so well. But then again, it's hard to believe that priests of some religions managed to make entire populations feel guilty for having sex, or to insist that only men could be leaders. Just as speaking in Latin can make the ridiculous seem plausible, so can talking in econobabble. Especially when the journalists nod along instead of asking politicians what on earth they are talking about.

WHERE DID THE BUDGET EMERGENCY GO?

Magicians know that the easiest things to make disappear are things that were never there. The only people who reported seeing a budget emergency are the same ones now assuring us it has moved on. So what happened?

Tony Abbott was elected on the 'magic pudding' platform of cutting taxes, not cutting spending and rapidly reducing the budget deficit. It was never going to happen. Ahead of the 2103 election, when pushed to promise not to break his impossible commitments, Mr Abbott did so:

> REPORTER: The condition of the budget will not be an excuse for breaking promises?
>
> TONY ABBOTT: Um, exactly right. We will make, we will keep the commitments that we make.[5]

When challenged on their decision in 2014 to introduce new taxes and cut spending which they had promised not to cut, Joe Hockey, entirely predictably, stated: 'Well, okay, if we are arguing what people said, gee whiz, I wish the other mob had told us how bad the budget was.'[6]

The political strategy was simple:

- Step 1: Cut a range of taxes (such as the carbon tax and the mining tax).

- Step 2: Hold a Commission of Audit to 'discover' that the budget was in 'worse shape' than expected.

- Step 3: Introduce cuts to welfare and government services on the basis that to do otherwise would be 'fiscally irresponsible'.

The right-wing ratchet was designed to work over decades, but Abbott and Hockey tried to jump from tax cuts to big business to co-payments and welfare cuts in less than six months. They were never going to get away with it.

In addition to their unseemly haste, the problem for the Abbott government was that while a majority of the Senate voted to cut taxes, a majority of senators could not be found to support cuts to the aged pension or a wide range of other proposed cuts. That's when things got interesting.

After spending the months following the 2014 budget thundering about the impending budget crisis and the need for the Senate to bow to the government's will, despite its lack of an electoral mandate, Joe Hockey finally began to realise that the Senate might not be bluffing. And, as he began to put together his second budget, he realised that in order to slay the 'budget emergency' he had told people existed, he might have to collect more tax revenue.

The then treasurer started to talk about the need to rein in the tax concessions for superannuation, which cost the budget tens of billions of dollars each year and flow almost entirely to the top half of earners. He talked of the need to collect more tax from multinational companies. And he even hinted at a new tax on the banks. Documents obtained under freedom of information legislation make clear that the Treasury was working on new revenue measures to fill the government's 'budget black hole'.

And then Peter Costello hit the roof. In a flurry of stinging articles, the former treasurer, and the architect of the twenty-year plan to 'starve the beast' in Australia, called on the Abbott government to cut taxes to fix the 'budget emergency'. Yep, you read that right. Peter Costello argued that 'the government needs to restart the conversation about getting taxes down, not up'.[7]

PROFLIGATE PETE AND THE TAX CUTS THAT BROKE THE BUDGET

Poor Joe Hockey. It wasn't his fault that Chinese demand for resources collapsed on his watch. Similarly, it wasn't his fault that the tax cuts and loopholes introduced by Peter Costello at the beginning of the mining boom have undermined the ability of our tax system to collect much revenue even when the economy is growing.

Joe Hockey's problem was the flipside of Costello's claim to be a 'great economic manager'. Put simply, the world economy has a much more significant impact on the 'performance' of Australian treasurers than Australian treasurers have on the world economy. But politics, like astrology, always needs to conflate causation with correlation. If it happened *after* I did something, it must have happened *because* of what I did.

It wasn't Gough Whitlam who caused the 1973 OPEC oil crisis and the collapse of the world economy. It wasn't Costello's budget surpluses that caused China to double its demand for our natural resources in the mid 2000s. And, despite what the Coalition argues, the meltdown of the global financial system and subsequent world recession in the late 2000s wasn't caused by Wayne Swan.

In reality, most of the movement in monthly economic indicators is driven by events beyond our borders, or by policy decisions made years earlier. Indeed, the budget emergency that once worried Joe Hockey had its genesis in the permanent tax cuts that Peter Costello introduced in response to a temporary spike in tax revenue at the beginning of the mining boom.

According to economists at the International Monetary Fund (IMF), Peter Costello was Australia's most profligate treasurer of the past fifty years.[8] That is, according to the global doyens of fiscal responsibility, the man described by John Howard as Australia's greatest treasurer spent like a drunken sailor when the economy was booming. In doing so, he poured fuel on the mining boom's fire, pushed up interest rates for those with mortgages, and helped cause the budget deficits that Joe Hockey was so worried about in 2014.

If Peter Costello was such a 'good economic manager', then how come in his time as treasurer we were never rich enough to give aged pensioners a pay rise, or to cut the price of medicine for sick people, or to invest heavily in renewable energy? Peter Costello gave away a fortune in tax cuts to the wealthy, and he simultaneously 'saved' billions of dollars by making the lives of the sick and the elderly harder than they needed to be. By his own criteria, that made him a 'great economic manager'. But by the IMF's definition it made him profligate and short-term. I prefer the adjectives the director of the Liberal Party used to describe the perception of Costello's government after the 2001 election: mean and tricky.[9]

BUT COSTELLO DELIVERED ELEVEN SURPLUSES IN A ROW!

Most people remember that Peter Costello delivered a string of budget surpluses. But what most people don't remember is that it was Peter Costello who convinced them that the definition of 'good economic management' was running a budget surplus. Even fewer people will admit that they have little idea what a budget surplus really means. Econobabble is used to conceal, not reveal.

Anyone who has ever bought a house or a new car has run a 'budget deficit'. If you earn $100,000 per year and buy a $700,000 house, you will rack up a big deficit that year and, inevitably, a big debt. Is that reckless or irresponsible? Most people, and most financial planners, don't think so. Nor do most companies.

Tony Shepherd, the man who ran the Abbott government's Commission of Audit, and who told the nation it had to live within its means, knows the value of debt better than most. During his time as chairman of Transfield, its debt ballooned from \$282 million to \$1.606 billion.[10]

Peter Costello played a simple trick on the Australian people during the Howard years. While economists see budget deficits and budget surpluses as tools to help manage the economy, 'Profligate Pete' redefined the budget outcome as the ultimate objective of economic management. Put simply, he convinced us that surpluses were good and deficits were bad. So if he delivered a surplus, he must have done a good job. Right? Wrong.

Costello squandered a mining boom and convinced millions that he'd saved the country. His enormous and inequitable tax cuts were so poorly timed that they forced the Reserve Bank to push up interest rates, which in turn cost middle-income earners with mortgages a fortune.

The existence of a budget surplus or deficit is not evidence of good or bad economic management. What does matter, however, is that the size of the surplus or deficit is appropriate for the economic conditions of the time, and that the composition of government spending sets the country up for the future. Costello used econobabble to conceal the complexity of the problems he faced, and to justify his simplistic goal to cut taxes for his friends and cut public spending on his foes.

In economic management, as in politics, timing is everything. While government budgets are an annual affair, economies have much longer cycles. All sorts of unexpected shocks – some good, some bad – affect our economy. And as the unexpected boom in China's demand for resources clearly shows, there are often many years between cause and effect.

The ups and downs of the Australian economy are known as the business cycle. While academic economists argue about definitions and measurement, the economy usually slows down every seven or eight years. By the middle of the 2000s Australia was about 'due' for a recession.[11] But we got lucky. Instead of a slowdown, we got the biggest resources boom we had seen in a century. The prices for our biggest exports rose rapidly, as did corporate profits and corporate tax receipts. The impacts were obviously good for the budget's bottom line.

But rather than stockpile this temporary increase in revenue, Costello introduced permanent tax cuts. He cut by half the tax payable on income from capital gains. He trebled the threshold for the top tax bracket. He made income from superannuation entirely tax-free, even for those who earned millions per year. He also handed out tens of billions of dollars' worth of benefits to middle- and high-income earners, while arguing that the government couldn't afford to increase unemployment benefits, disability benefits or the aged pension.

The windfall revenue from the mining boom was so great that, despite Costello's largesse, the budget was still in surplus. With repetition, and with vocal support from a cheer squad of 'business leaders', he convinced people that simply delivering a surplus proved that he was doing a great job.

But the idea that a budget surplus is proof of good policy has no basis in economics. Imagine an ice-cream shop in a small beach resort. In the summer months it does a roaring trade; in the winter months it's a nice quiet place for the staff to read. Now imagine that you are the owner of the shop. In the middle of a long and hot summer, you see an ad for the car of your dreams. With ice-cream sales at record highs, you would still be in surplus even after the enormous monthly repayments. Would you buy the car on that basis?

According to the pinko lefties at the IMF, Peter Costello hosed our mining boom up against a wall. Indeed, according to the Reserve Bank of Australia, Costello's tax cuts and middle-class welfare pumped so much money back into the booming economy of the late 2000s that he forced it to increase interest rates to 'take the heat' out of the economy.[12] (That's another nasty economic phrase that not enough people understand. When the RBA says it is increasing interest rates to 'take the heat' out of the economy, what it really means is 'increase everybody's mortgage repayments to lower their disposable income in the hope that they spend less money in the shops and cause a bit of unemployment'.)

Tens of billions of dollars' worth of tax cuts and new benefits were pumped back into an economy that was already booming. Virtually all economists agree that such fiscal stimulus when the economy is already booming is the exact opposite of responsible economic management. Theory and history say such stimulus would push up inflation and interest rates. Which is exactly what happened. He could have poured the money into the infrastructure a rapidly growing population would need, which would have boosted both short-term employment and long-term productivity growth, but he gave it to his friends as inflationary tax cuts instead.

Costello must have known his tax cuts and middle-class spending splurge were economically irresponsible. Treasury told him, the RBA told him, the IMF told him. But he wasn't doing economic policy; he was doing politics. He owned the ice-cream shop during a hot summer and gave away free ice-cream to all his friends. The books looked okay during his tenure, but all the freebies meant that the coming winter would be long and impoverished.

Costello didn't want to manage the Australian economy; he wanted to permanently reshape Australian society – to shrink the public sector and let the market provide more of our health, education and welfare services. All the things that, more recently, Tony Abbott and Tony Shepherd said we had to do. But to achieve his vision, Costello had to cause budget deficits in the future, deficits big enough to scare the public into accepting big cuts to the services and safety nets that Australians are quite proud of. While it was easy for Costello to sell the tax cuts during the boom, the big cuts in spending in the future would be a tougher sell. That task fell to Joe Hockey, and he failed at the first hurdle. Now it's Scott Morrison's turn.

SO IS DEBT GOOD OR BAD?

Like a budget deficit, debt is neither good nor bad. It's just debt. What can be thought of as good or bad are the decisions we make about what it is worth borrowing money to fund, and what things we might miss out on because of our reluctance to borrow.

Debt simply allows us to bring expenditure forward in time. If we bring forward good ideas, we can increase our future income. If we bring forward bad ideas, then when we repay the money with interest we will have less to spend in the future. Again, it is not debt that is good or bad – what matters is the assets we are investing in, or missing out on.

Consider the following:

- A young person could work until they have saved up enough money to pay up front for their uni degree and then graduate with no debt. Or they could borrow the cost of their degree and go to uni ten years earlier.

- A young family could rent until they have saved up the full price of a house and buy a home with no debt. Or they could save up a deposit, take out a mortgage and buy a home decades earlier.

- A small business owner could save up all of the funds
  needed to open a new store in a new location. Or they
  could borrow money against the existing business,
  and set up the new shop years earlier.

What all three of the above scenarios have in common is
that debt allows the borrower to bring a good idea forward.
The cost of bringing a good idea forward is the interest we
pay on the borrowed funds. And the benefits of bringing a
good idea forward in the above examples are:

- Swifter access to a high-paid job.

- The ability to avoid rent and to accumulate capital
  gain on a house.

- Earlier access to the flow of profit that will come from
  opening a new shop.

Economics 101 does not teach us that 'debt is bad'. Rather,
it suggests that a rational decision-maker should always
pursue options in which the benefits exceed the costs.

But let's think about the alternative. If we agree with
the idea that debt is simply bad, then the determination
to avoid debt would lead us to avoid good investments
whose returns would far exceed the cost of interest.
The desire to be 'debt-free' would lead us to accumulate
fewer of the assets we need for future prosperity. Such an
app-roach has become synonymous with 'good politics',
but it is entirely unrelated to notions of 'good economic

decision-making' – except in the minds of those who, like Peter Costello, believe that all public spending is a bad idea.

The pursuit of 'deficit reduction' as an end in itself would lead governments to:

- Avoid all investment in effective preventative health measures.

- Cut all spending on schools and higher education.

- Endure the costs of climate change rather than invest in things that might prevent them.

- Sell all public assets – even those that pay dividends of 10 per cent.

Households that want simply to 'repay debt' can do so – by selling their homes. Indeed, by Joe Hockey's logic, parents with a mortgage who send their kids to expensive private schools should stop doing so and direct all their funds towards repaying their home loan. But these parents presumably believe that the benefits of investing in their children's education are worth much more than the interest they pay on their mortgage. It's a pity more politicians don't think like that.

Just as conservatives define 'good economic management' as running a budget surplus, they claim that 'reducing debt' should be a goal of government policy. Using hackneyed and fundamentally flawed household analogies about 'living within your means', Peter Costello, Tony Abbott and Joe Hockey made their failure to invest in Australia's future look like evidence of their concern for future generations.

GOVERNMENTS SHOULD BORROW MORE THAN HOUSEHOLDS, NOT LESS

The average household in Australia has total debts of around \$230,000. As a proportion of household income, on average Australian households carry 150 per cent debt. The net debt that the government holds on our behalf, however, accounts for only 17 per cent of our national income. That's down from 41 per cent when Menzies left office. The OECD average, meanwhile, is 51 per cent.[13]

It makes sense for households to aim to repay most of their debts before they retire. For most Australians, retirement means that the most expensive stages of life (buying a house and raising kids) have passed. And most retirees' income falls when they leave the workforce (only the very rich and the unemployed get a pay rise when they turn sixty-five). But when will Australia retire?

Despite decades of our being told otherwise, nation-states are not like households in any significant sense. Unless a government plans for Australia to retire at some point soon, then it makes no economic sense to repay all the nation's debts by some arbitrary deadline. Of course debt means that interest payments must be made, but as with a HECS debt or a mortgage, what is relevant is whether the benefits the nation has gained exceed those costs.

Far from retiring, Australia is growing very rapidly. Some 4 million people move to Australia each decade, and so the need for new investment in schools, roads, hospitals, trains, police stations and sewers is enormous. Indeed, the budgetary cost of population growth far exceeds the cost of population ageing.[14]

Schools, roads and sewers last for decades. Indeed, as the Romans showed, if built well, roads will deliver benefits to future taxpayers for centuries. So why should this generation of taxpayers bear the whole cost – by paying cash up front – for infrastructure that will deliver benefits to many generations to come? Why should the cost of building new schools and hospitals come out of existing funding for teachers and nurses?

That's what 'starving the beast' is all about. To Peter Costello, Joe Hockey and Tony Shepherd, our schools, hospitals, aged care homes and public transport system are 'the beast'. While other countries are investing heavily in education, renewable energy and public transport, Australia is cutting back. Someone is going in the wrong direction.

CONCLUSION

As we've seen, cutting taxes when the economy is booming is not 'good economic management' – it's really irresponsible. Even the RBA and IMF admit that pouring tax cuts into a booming economy (instead of funding infrastructure bottlenecks) drives up inflation and interest rates. By cutting taxes, however, the Coalition has managed to convince the public that even though we live in one of the richest countries in the world, we can't afford to invest in our children or provide high-quality care for our elderly.

Running a surplus isn't 'proof' of good economic management, but if you can convince the public it is, then you will have a much easier time convincing them that investing in the infrastructure a rapidly growing population needs is 'irresponsible'. And if you can persuade the public that they should fund the next 100 years' worth of infrastructure out of the budget for today's teachers and nurses, cutting the quality of public services becomes easier still.

Econobabble can make rich countries feel poor. Amazingly, it can also make cutting taxes for the rich while cutting spending on the poor seem 'economically responsible'.

Words matter.

CHAPTER 5
THE TRUTH ABOUT THE FREE MARKET

Big businesses are built on red tape and regulation. They love it. The big banks, the big miners and the big software companies wouldn't be big without it. Indeed, big business loves regulation so much that their balance sheets often record the value of it as an 'asset'. Regulation helps to keep competitors out and prices up. Regulation limits the claims for damages that employees and customers can make against companies, and, of course, regulation forces us to buy products that many of us don't want. Without regulation, the legal, accounting and lobbying businesses wouldn't exist.

But econobabble about the 'horrors of red tape' and 'the need for regulatory certainty' allows business groups, and their apologists in parliament and the media, to walk both sides of a pretty wide street. When businesses oppose a regulation because it will cost them money, they use terms like 'red tape', 'nanny state' and 'individual choice'. They almost inevitably talk about the 'burden' and the 'cost' of regulation, and (as discussed in Chapter Seven) often produce reports with absurdly precise estimates of the alleged 'cost to the economy' of the laws they don't like.

But when businesses like a regulation because it will make them money, the econobabble takes on quite a different accent. In that case, strong economies are based on 'stable regulation' or, intriguingly, 'responsive regulation'. *Responsive* is just econobabble for 'governments should do what we tell them to'.

Put simply, the costs and benefits of regulation are in the eye of the beholder. And the role of econobabble is to make some beholders seem more credible than others. Apparently, when 'the markets' say we need regulation, governments should listen, but when the voters demand it, governments should 'resist populism'.

In the debate about the size and shape of regulation in Australia, the strategy of business groups is pretty simple: they privately love the regulations they love, and they publicly hate the regulations they hate. It's much easier for business groups to pretend to hate all regulation, and to pretend that all regulation will 'cost jobs' and 'reduce confidence', than it is to win a public debate about which kinds of regulation are in the national interest, and which are simply in the interests of the businesses demanding them.

Don't believe me? Consider this. The business community is forever calling for 'labour market deregulation', and in 2006 the Howard government delivered them the WorkChoices legislation – which amounted to 1000 pages of regulation. It took a lot of new regulation to deregulate the labour market, but the business community was happy nonetheless. Business groups don't hate all regulation – they just hate the regulations they hate.

BUSINESSES LOVE THE REGULATIONS THAT FORCE US TO BUY THEIR PRODUCTS

Australians are forced by government regulation to spend 9.5 per cent of their income buying superannuation. In fact, the average Australian household spends more money each year on superannuation *fees* than it does on electricity.[1] Of course, the premise underlying compulsory superannuation is that individuals can't be trusted to make their own decisions – but you don't hear the finance industry complaining about the way that regulation is 'stifling freedom'.

The superannuation industry, which prides itself on the bewildering array of 'choice' it offers consumers, will never support the removal of the laws that force all working Australians to buy their products. It's one thing to make customers choose between tens of thousands of superannuation products, but letting people decide for themselves how much superannuation they want to contribute when they are saving up to buy a house – that's going way too far.

It's a similar story with private health insurance, which Australians who earn above average incomes are effectively forced to buy. In this case, of course, you can 'choose' to not buy private health insurance, but if you do make that choice you have to pay an extra 1 per cent in income tax for those singles on $90,000 per annum (sliding up to 1.5 per cent for higher income earners) – an amount which is more than the cost of a cheap private health insurance policy.[2] Again, it is rare to hear the private health insurers complain about regulation and the need to 'empower' individuals to make their own choices.

Licensed electricians support regulations that prevent amateurs from wiring their own houses; pharmacists love regulations that prevent new pharmacies being built within 1.5 kilometres of their shops; coal-seam gas companies love the regulations that permit them to drill on farmers' land even if the farmers don't want to allow it.

REGULATION IS A GREAT IDEA, AND ECONOMIES COULDN'T WORK WITHOUT IT

None of this is to say that regulation is a bad idea – it's not. Banning asbestos was a good idea. Banning cigarette advertising was a good idea. Taking lead out of petrol was a great idea. And I am yet to meet a libertarian who thinks that anyone who wants to call themselves a surgeon should be free to do so.

The self-described 'ultra-libertarian' Senator David Leyonhjelm claims to be so concerned about regulation that he actually set up a taxpayer-funded inquiry into the 'nanny state'.[2] Yet he also wants to ban wind turbines because of the 'infrasound' they generate.[3] A genuine libertarian would tell the tiny minority of people who are bothered by the infrasound to sell their houses to members of the vast majority who can't hear it.

Our economy, and indeed our society, literally couldn't function without regulation. While history and international observation tells us that it is possible to create healthy and wealthy societies with an enormous range of regulation, economics cannot actually tell us which regulations are 'best'. Decisions about the kind of regulations we want are ultimately decisions about the kind of society we want. They are expressions of our values and our objectives, and so are best made democratically. That's why business groups work so hard to dress them up in econobabble – to ensure they aren't made democratically.

Business groups know perfectly well what the answer would be if citizens were asked: 'Do you think factories should be free to pollute our air and water?' Econobabble allows a skilled business lobbyist or politician to reframe the question: 'Keeping in mind the importance of maintaining our competitive advantage, would you support additional regulations on Australian businesses if it resulted in higher costs to producers and consumers?'

REGULATION IS EVERYWHERE, AND THAT'S A GOOD THING

Most people don't want poo on their food. Or cockroaches in commercial kitchens. Or meat that hasn't been kept in a fridge. That's why nearly everybody supports the regulation of the food industry. Everyone except those parts of the food industry that 'keep costs down' by importing the odd bit of food with poo on it.

Car companies are forced to install seat belts in all cars sold in Australia. But the red tape doesn't stop there: we also force people to wear them, and we pay police to check if people are complying. And if they aren't, we force them to pay a fine. In a true 'free market', car companies would choose whether to install seat belts or not, customers would choose whether they wanted to buy cars with seat belts or not, and passengers would decide whether to wear seat belts or not. And in a society free of 'burdensome' regulation, we could all drive on either side of the road – or even the footpath – in cars that lacked not only seat belts but mufflers as well. Such a scenario is obviously ridiculous. In a society that had no taxes or regulation, there would be no roads to drive on anyway.

There is no evidence to support the idea that individuals left to their own devices always make decisions that are in their own best interests, let alone in the community's best interests. Not even Adam Smith, the man who gave us the concept of the 'invisible hand', believed we needed no regulation. Consider the following:

- Should your neighbours be allowed to make as much noise as they want at any time they want?

- Should factories be able to dispose of their untreated pollution into the air or water whenever they want?

- Should shops be able to sell products that fall apart within days of purchase?

- Should food producers be allowed to conceal the ingredients they include in the food they sell?

If you answered 'no' to any of the above questions, then obviously you are a red-tape-loving nanny-statist who wants to stifle innovation and individual responsibility by creating more burdensome regulation. Either that or you're a sensible adult.

A favourite right-wing debating trick is to push people into accepting one of two extreme, and ridiculous, positions. For example, do you think that red tape is ruining the world, or do you think that individuals are better than bureaucrats at deciding how to live their lives? Are you with us or against us?

The best strategy is to respond in kind. Do shock-jocks think we should let hoodlums make as much noise as they want at any time, or should we implement tough laws (regulations) to ensure that hard-working citizens can get some rest at night? (If you haven't noticed, most shock-jocks claim to hate 'nanny-state regulation', but they simultaneously claim to love 'law and order'.)

In reality, regulation is always a compromise. Some regulations are stupid, and some do stifle innovation. But that doesn't stop the taxi industry from demanding regulatory protection from ride-sharing companies like Uber that use new technology to match people with cars to people who want a lift. And it doesn't stop music companies wanting tougher 'laws' to imprison and fine people who share movies or music with their friends. It's not only environmentalists and fussy consumer groups who can be accused of supporting dumb regulations which stifle innovation.

BUSINESSES DON'T WANT TO BE 'COMPETITIVE', THEY WANT TO BE MONOPOLISTS

One of the most shocking conclusions of economic theory is that in an efficient market, firms barely make a profit. That is, when a market is genuinely 'competitive' – in the economists' sense of the word – and has many buyers and sellers, none of whom have market power and all of whom are selling similar products, no individual firm will ever make a large profit.

It gets weirder. In the land of the economics textbook, the land econobabblers pretend to know well, firms earning large profits are a sign that something is *wrong* with the market. Large profits are in fact evidence of 'market failure'. Indeed, economists think that large profits should only ever be a temporary problem, as the profit itself would act as a signal to other firms to enter the market. New entrants, possibly using new technologies, should be able to push prices and profits down, and restore the market to its competitive (low-profit) state (which economists call *equilibrium*).

The way the pursuit of profit destroys profit is a big part of Adam Smith's 'invisible hand', and it's why economists love the idea of 'free markets'. Businesspeople, on the other hand, don't actually like free markets and healthy competition for the same reason that economists do like those things: genuine competition reduces the likelihood of profits.

For a company to maintain high levels of profitability, it needs to be able to prevent new competitors from entering the market. Economists call things that keep new entrants out of a market 'barriers to entry'; businesspeople call them by many names, including:

- Licences (the taxi, casino and television industries are built on them).

- Patents (Apple tried to keep Samsung out of the tablet computer market by claiming they owned the idea of a rectangular screen).

- Copyrights.

- Trademarks.

- Joint marketing boards (such as the Australian Wheat Board).

- Geographical Indications (for instance, that champagne can only be produced by winemakers from the Champagne region of France).

While businesses use a wide and contradictory array of econobabble to justify the need for the barriers to entry that protect their profits, they can be summarised with the word the business community is determined not to use: *regulation*.

There is simply no such thing as a 'free market'. Nowhere. For anything. All markets are regulated in some way. Unfortunately, the nonsensical debate about whether we should regulate markets or not is used by the econobabblers to crowd out a more interesting and important conversation about which kinds of regulation are good for society and which kinds are not. While there will be no simple answer to that question, a national debate would likely yield far better outcomes for consumers, citizens, the environment and even the economy. There would probably be losers, too, but in a free market that is exactly what is supposed to happen.

While trained economists assume that profits are a signal for new firms to enter an industry and push prices down for consumers, in Australia profits are used to build barriers to entry to keep competitors out and prices up. And the cheapest and most effective are regulatory barriers. Let's consider some examples.

The taxi industry

Taxis in most Australians capital cities are expensive, slow, unreliable and smelly. They are also very, very profitable. But if you own a reliable car, have a driver's licence, are keen to drive people around and are looking for work, don't bother trying to enter the taxi industry unless you also have a spare $300,000 in the bank. That is the cost of a taxi licence in Sydney. To put it another way, that's the size of the barrier that you have to hurdle if you want to enter the industry. If you want to 'compete' with the current taxi fleet, you first have to pay for the privilege. Think about that: you have to pay your competitor for the right to compete with them. So much for 'free markets'.

Technological change often overcomes the barriers behind which profitable monopolists and oligopolists hide. Google destroyed the profits of the *Yellow Pages*. eBay destroyed the profitability of classified advertisements. And GPS units have destroyed the profits of the street directory publishers. But the taxi industry isn't going to go quietly. They can see the barbarians at the regulatory gate, and they are spending enormous amounts of their customers' money to solidify the regulatory barriers that protect their enormous profits.

Hire cars have always provided some competition to taxis, but only when the consumer planned ahead. The bizarre but effective laws that protect the owners of taxi licences specifically prevent 'hire cars' from picking people up off the street. You can only use them if you book in advance. Similarly, paying your mate some 'petrol money' for a lift home has always been legal. But both hire cars and organising for a friend to drive take foresight, which, historically, has left the taxi industry with a monopoly on providing last-minute rides. Technological change now allows us to 'book' an Uber car one minute before we need it, or find a 'friend' online willing to drive us somewhere for money.

Where customers see convenience, the taxi industry sees competition. And when profits are under serious threat, the first thing thrown overboard is the rhetoric of free markets.

As ride-sharing companies like Uber have set up in cities around the world, the owners of Australia's taxis have not responded by making their service cleaner, cheaper or more reliable. Experience tells the taxi industry that the best way to see off competition is to desperately chase stronger regulation that will keep the new competitors out. But of course the explanation the taxi companies give for doing this has nothing to do with their profits – they simply want to 'protect their customers'.

The pharmacists

In 2012 two pharmacists proposed opening a new store in the Canberra suburb of Hackett, but it was quickly derided as a crazy idea. Given that there was already a chemist 1.5 kilometres away, in the suburb of Watson, there was clearly no need for a new one in Hackett. Anyone who has read the federal government's 'Pharmacy Agreement' knows that a new pharmacy cannot be opened within 1.5 kilometres of an existing one. Imagine if there were two near each other! Competing! Where would it end?

The Pharmacy Guild of Australia is one of the country's most powerful unions. In fact, it is so powerful that it is considered impolite to call it a union. It's a guild – and don't you forget it.

The pharmacists' union has one of the biggest buildings of all the lobbyists who can afford to have a permanent physical presence in Canberra's very expensive 'Parliamentary triangle'. You might think it is odd for a bunch of small-business owners to take Canberra lobbying and the need for 'stable regulation' so seriously, but the fact is that every Australian pharmacy has a local monopoly on the distribution of billions of dollars' worth of taxpayer-subsidised medicine each year. It's a very nice little earner.

The regulations banning new shops from setting up don't just protect pharmacists from competition, they also ensure that young pharmacists have no choice but to work for the incumbents rather than set up on their own.

One day, if they are lucky, the young chemists can pay millions of dollars to buy one of the restricted number of pharmacies, from someone whose business has been protected from competition for decades. While pharmacies usually smell a bit better than taxis, the laws that protect them both stink.

We could 'let the market decide' how many pharmacists an area can support. We could allow supermarkets to employ trained pharmacists, and let them dispense drugs; this is what happens in most countries. Or we could stick with the status quo.

The pharmacy industry, like the taxi industry, is adamant that the existing regulations are there to protect customers, not pharmacy owners. That's a relief.

Free-to-air television

For decades, Australians had access to only three commercial free-to-air television stations because the government had decided to issue only three licences. That, we were told, was the right number. Granting only two licences would not have allowed for enough 'competition', and granting four licences would be unsustainable – and we wouldn't want to see an entrepreneur try to set up a fourth channel and go broke. It's better to protect people from themselves.

As Australia's population grew, and the total advertising revenue of the three commercial television stations grew faster still, it seemed that three remained the right number of channels. Without their big profits, we were told, the commercial television stations couldn't afford to make Australian drama. Restricting the number of commercial television licences was the best way to both protect and promote Australian culture.

But then something strange happened. As more and more people began to use mobile phones and wireless internet services, the 'electromagnetic spectrum' in which phone, internet, radio and television signals are broadcast began to get crowded. A partial solution to this congestion was to move television broadcasts to new channels, which, when combined with the switch from analogue to digital transmission, meant there was now the possibility of around forty free-to-air television stations.

So what is the right number of free-to-air commercial television licences now? You will never guess: it's still three.

It turned out that, despite our capacity to admit new broadcasters to the Australian television market, the best way to give Australians 'choice' was to let the three owners of the existing licences decide what else we can see. And their decision – which was largely to put more info-mercials and repeats to air – speaks volumes.

Commercial television licenses are worth hundreds of millions of dollars. And just like in the taxi industry and the pharmacy industry, if you want to enter the television market you have to pay one of the incumbents for the privilege.

SO DO WE NEED MORE REGULATION OR LESS?

'The challenge is to strike the right balance between appropriate safety standards and consumer access to vehicles at the lowest price. Policy options are still being considered and it is expected the marketplace will play a role in providing consumers with options to mitigate the risks of overseas purchases.'

—JAMIE BRIGGS, ASSISTANT MINISTER FOR INFRASTRUCURE AND REGIONAL DEVELOPMENT, 2015[4]

Try to decode the above quote. I can't. Despite their rhetoric about deregulation, most free-marketeers, when pushed for their position on regulations that protect the profits of existing companies, head straight for the econobabble. The above quotation, for example, is an attempt by the Honourable Jamie Briggs MP to answer the question of whether we should make it easier to import second-hand cars. His reference to 'the marketplace playing a role' was a nice touch, given that the question was whether or not *the parliament* would change the regulations.

To recap, the idea that business owners want truly 'free markets' and open 'competition' is as absurd as it is widely repeated. Regulation is the most powerful weapon in the corporate arsenal, and the purpose of all the money spent by companies on lobbying, PR and political donations is to ensure that, whoever is in government, the regulations that enable their profits are protected and enhanced.

Throughout the 1990s and 2000s, the 'economic rationalists' raged against red tape and regulation. They mounted a noisy and effective campaign opposed to regulation and in support of free markets. It was not an accident that their calls focused on the need to privatise government services and 'deregulate' the labour market. And it was no accident that the need to 'deregulate' pharmacies, taxis, television and gambling never appeared on their to-do list.

WHY DIVESTMENT DIVIDES THE RIGHT

Despite their 'libertarian' values when it comes to the corporate world, most conservatives usually abandon the cause of freedom when it comes to our personal lives. Nowhere is the hypocrisy of the political Right more obvious than in the arbitrary line they draw between 'economic issues' and 'social issues'. Indeed, many right-wingers want a government that is just small enough to fit into your bedroom.

Consider the recent controversies around 'divestment'. The divestment movement is a worldwide campaign aimed at encouraging individuals, community organisations, universities, investment funds and companies to sell their shares in businesses that are engaged in activities inconsistent with the shareholders' values. While the most visible divestment campaigns in the world today revolve around concerns about climate change – they encourage the sale of shares in fossil-fuel companies – a wide range of other environmental and human rights campaigns are also being conducted.

Divestment campaigns pose an existential threat to the political compromise between 'market liberals' and 'social conservatives'. Consider the following:

- For decades, market liberals have chosen to focus on the 'deregulation' of markets, but have been largely silent about 'values issues', such as freedoms in relation to homosexual sex, same-sex marriage, euthanasia, abortion or the prohibition of recreational drugs.

- For decades, 'social conservatives' have chosen to focus on 'values issues' related to sexuality, drugs and death, while remaining largely silent about 'social justice' issues such as the gap between rich and poor, the adequacy of the social safety net, and the need for decent wages and conditions.

The business community and conservative churches have spent decades behaving like pharmacists and staying off each other's turf, but now divestment campaigns are bringing the world of money and the world of social values crashing into each other.

Consumers are trained daily to believe that the things they own say something about them. The cars, clothes, perfume and watches we own are all, we are told, a reflection of ourselves. But while many progressives have raged against the idea that 'we are what we own', in recent times campaigners such as Bill McKibben have shifted the public debate, arguing that if we are what we own, we shouldn't own shares in companies which profit from activities that are inconsistent with our values.

The significance of the political and philosophical threat posed by the divestment movement was on full display in the Abbott government's response to the Australian National University's decision to divest itself of a small bundle of shares in mining companies. The education minister and the Minerals Council of Australia raged against the decision. The then prime minister said the decision was 'stupid'.[5]

During the kerfuffle, the Australia Institute took out a full-page advertisement in the *Australian Financial Review*, pointing out:

- that capitalism is built on the notion that shareholders can sell their shares whenever they want; and

- that the government was simultaneously suggesting the leadership of the ANU was making 'stupid' investment decisions, and that (if the government's proposed deregulation of university fees happened) those same 'stupid' people would be setting the prices of university degrees.

While divestment campaigns alone will never be sufficient to tackle climate change, end child labour or ensure gender pay equality, there is little doubt that they can raise awareness of these issues as well as give individuals a way to put their money where their mouth is. They play an important role in 'making room' for regulatory solutions.

If the business and political leaders who claim to have so much faith in freedom and individual choice meant a word of what they said, they would have endorsed the divestment movement for what it is: individuals expressing their desires through the market.

But the words of most business leaders about free markets, individual choice and the power of market forces are just econobabble. They've been carefully selected to mean nothing, and to crowd out real democratic debates about what we should regulate and how we should go about it.

CHAPTER 6
THE MYTH OF FREE TRADE

Free-trade agreements are the most deceptive and misleading product since the mining industry told the world that 'clean coal' would tackle climate change. The American government is determined to restrict imports of sugar, the Japanese government is determined to restrict imports of rice and the Australian government claims to have free-trade agreements with both of them!

There is no such thing as free trade, and no country on the planet is pursuing it as a goal. So-called free-trade agreements are actually nothing of the sort. The document known as the *Australia–United States Free Trade Agreement* is over 1000 pages long, but you should be able to sum it up in one line: 'There will be no restrictions on trade between Australia and the United States.' What those thousand pages in fact do is spell out all the mutually agreeable restrictions on trade. As people have gradually caught on to the fact that free-trade agreements are nothing of the sort, governments have tried to rebrand them. Take the Trans-Pacific Partnership, for example. Who could be opposed to a 'partnership'?

Trade isn't good or bad – it is simply trade. All countries impose rules on trade to protect their customers, industries or geopolitical interests. Conservative politicians have created a phoney debate about 'free trade' in order to conceal what they are really up to: redefining the rules of trade in ways that are good for people they like and bad for those they don't like.

WHAT WOULD REAL FREE TRADE LOOK LIKE?

Despite our so-called free-trade agreement with the United States, Australian residents can't download music or movies from US companies on the same terms as American residents – we get them later and at higher prices. The US sellers use 'geo-blocking' software to ensure that Australian consumers can't freely trade with them. Here are a few examples:

- Apple charges Australian consumers more to download Australian music from iTunes than it charges Americans to purchase the same songs.

- The jeweller Tiffany sells exactly the same pieces to Americans at significant lower prices than they charge Australians. If an Australian goes to the US website and tries to pay the US price, they are redirected to the more expensive Australian website.

- Netflix charges Australians higher prices than it charges US residents, and often cannot make programs available to Australians until months after US residents have seen them.

Those arguing for an Australia–US free trade agreement claimed it would give Australians greater choice at lower prices. But now that the agreement is in place, they're conspicuously silent about the inability of Australian consumers to access these benefits.

NO COUNTRY WANTS FREE TRADE

Like most countries, Australia encourages other nations to embrace free trade, but we are deeply reluctant to do so ourselves. Of course, while other countries are motivated solely by short-sighted and selfish 'protectionism', Australia's trade restrictions have no such base motives. Consider the following:

- We want Japan to abolish its restrictions on importing rice, but we restrict the importing of bananas.

- We want the United States to lift its restrictions on importing our sugar, but we won't allow fresh chicken meat to be imported into Australia.

- We want Indonesia to relax its restrictions on Australian meat, but we plan to keep our extensive restrictions on the importing of second-hand cars.

Fortunately, in my view at least, Australian citizens can't freely import assault rifles from the United States because Australian trade restrictions prevent it. Again, trade isn't good or bad – it's just trade. It's citizens who distinguish good from bad, not economists or trade negotiators. Unfortunately, however, all the econobabble about 'free trade' being 'good for the economy' has stopped us from having a much-needed debate about which restrictions on trade are good and which ones are not.

Australian and US trade negotiators do have conversations about this sort of thing – in private – but the phoney language of 'free trade versus protectionism' keeps the population out of it. Our trade negotiators therefore make all the important decisions without justifying themselves to the people whose interests they supposedly serve.

AMERICANS AREN'T AFRAID OF GUNS BUT THEY ARE AFRAID OF CHEESE

Americans, as we all know, are a bunch of freedom-loving, risk-taking, rugged individualists whose only fear related to guns is that they don't have enough of them. Americans don't need nanny-state regulations to protect them from armour-piercing bullets. The Constitution gives them all the protection they need ... but not enough protection from unpasteurised cheese.

Even freedom-loving, risk-taking Americans aren't irresponsible. They might know that guns don't kill people, but they also know that unpasteurised cheese will. And while thousands of kids are killed by guns in the United States each year, one kid dying from listeria from unpasteurised French cheese is, it seems, just too big a risk to take. That's why they ban the importing of raw-milk Camembert, Brie, goat's cheese and a wide range of other dairy products. A cynic might argue that the American dairy industry wants protection from high-quality French imports.

Don't get me wrong – maybe it's a great idea to ban unpasteurised cheese imports. I'm an economist, not an epidemiologist, and I know next to nothing about bacterial infections. But I do know BS when I hear it. And you don't need to be an epidemiologist or an economist to spot the fundamental and glaring inconsistencies in the arguments that are used to support 'free trade' for some things and 'protection' for others.

AMERICANS CAN MAKE CHAMPAGNE, BUT THEY CAN'T SELL IT TO AUSTRALIANS

Australian winemakers once produced champagne, but they are no longer allowed to. The French won't let them, so these days Australian winemakers produce 'sparkling wine'. The use of the term *champagne* provides an interesting example of the tension between two assumptions in the idea of 'perfect competition', upon which so much policy is based.

One assumption is that of 'perfect information'. To put it another way, it's assumed that consumers always know what they are buying and so can never be ripped off. It's a pretty heroic assumption to make. Clear labelling laws can help consumers, so insisting that only wineries in the Champagne region can sell champagne is, arguably, a pro-consumer attempt to make sure people know what they are buying.

However, another of the assumptions that underpins the belief in free markets says that 'there are no barriers to entry'. What this means is that there is nothing that will stop new wineries (or factories or anything else) from supplying similar products.

So we have two competing priorities – consumer protection and free trade – and weighing them is a highly political and subjective exercise. What's more, the decisions are made by politicians who are usually under a lot of pressure from an industry lobbyist or seven. History suggests that politicians would much prefer to conduct such balancing acts behind closed doors – perhaps because the ultimate decision usually has far more to do with bargaining and lobbying power than it does with economic efficiency or consumer protection.

Now, are you ready for your head to explode? Did you know that although Australian winemakers aren't allowed to make champagne because they aren't from the Champagne region of France, Californian winemakers are? The reason is simply that America has a lot more bargaining power than Australia.

The US market is a lot more important to French wine exporters than the Australian market is, and the French didn't want to get into a trade war with the United States. What the French saw as 'matters of principle' when negotiating with Australia became 'matters of market size' when dealing with the Americans.

The idea that some product names can only be used by producers from a particular region is known in trade law circles as Geographical Indication (GI). It effectively creates a brand that can only be used by producers who come from a particular area. Everyone knows about wine regions such as Champagne and Bordeaux, but other examples include Stilton and Roquefort cheese. It seems simple, but in fact it's not.

We know that Australia has a 'free-trade agreement' with the United States, which is supposed to mean that there are no restrictions on trade between our two countries. And we now know that while American winemakers can call their sparkling wine *champagne*, Australian wine-makers can't. So can an American winemaker export its champagne to Australia? No chance. The 'free-trade agreement' between the United States and the European Union specifically bans US companies from exporting anything called 'champagne' to Australia.

It gets worse. Deals between individual countries are called 'bilateral' agreements while those among multiple countries are called 'multilateral' agreements – examples of the latter are the North American Free Trade Agreement (NAFTA) and the Trans-Pacific Partnership (TPP). Not only do rules in some bilateral deals override rules in some multilateral deals, but sometimes rules in multilateral agreements can override rules in bilateral agreements.

There is nothing 'free' about the interlocking set of bi-lateral and multilateral trade agreements that regulate trade between countries. Indeed, companies that can't af-ford teams of lawyers to help them navigate the overlapping regulatory nets have no chance of competing with those companies that can.

Even the 'free marketeers' at the Productivity Com-mission have been critical of the current approach to trade agreements. It refuses to use the term *free-trade agree-ments*, preferring the more accurate *preferential-trade agreements*. In a 2015 report it stated: 'Preferential trade agreements add to the complexity and cost of interna-tional trade through substantially different sets of rules of origin, varying coverage of services and potentially costly intellectual property protections and investor-state dispute settlement provisions.' Five years earlier it noted that 'businesses have provided little evidence that Australia's [bilateral trade agreements] have generated significant commercial benefits'.[1]

Needless to say, despite the Commission's concerns, neither the bureaucrats at the Department of Trade nor the business groups that usually rage against such bureaucrats have expressed any worry that these agreements are stifling trade for the small businesses that are struggling to navigate the byzantine and overlapping set of rules Australia now has.

SO IF FREE TRADE DOESN'T EXIST, WHY DO SO MANY POWERFUL PEOPLE PRETEND TO WANT IT?

Hitler's propaganda chief, Joseph Goebbels, said that if you're going to tell a lie, you should make it a big one. What we call free-trade agreements are really the exact opposite. The long and complicated deals actually promise to treat some countries, and some industries, differently. To call such an abuse of language 'Orwellian' overstates Orwell's foresight. Free-trade agreements primarily deliver benefits to the industry groups that are powerful enough to shape them. There are three main reasons countries pursue free-trade agreements; let's examine them in turn.

1. Free-trade agreements provide powerful images.

While it may seem trite, a major benefit of signing a free-trade agreement with the United States or China is the photo opportunity that comes with it. The leaders of large and powerful countries know this and use it to their advantage in negotiations. Do you think the US media paid as much attention to signing a free-trade agreement with Australia as the Australian press did? What Australian prime ministers might call a defining moment in our relationship with a powerful country is no more than a footnote in theirs. (Sometimes literally so: George W. Bush's biography made only three passing references to John Howard, including a footnote, while Howard dedicated large slabs of his autobiography to his relationship with Bush.)

While Australian politicians suggest our free-trade agreement with the United States makes us special, in fact the Americans have signed twenty such 'special' agreements with countries as diverse as Honduras, Jordan, Peru and Canada. They're currently pursuing thirteen more, in order to strengthen their 'special' relationships with Mozambique, Mauritius and the United Arab Emirates, among others.

2. Free-trade agreements are weapons in the domestic political war.

The opaque nature of trade negotiations allows negotiators enormous latitude to pursue benefits for their political friends and impose pain on industries or constituencies to which they are hostile or indifferent.

For example, despite the fact that agriculture accounts for only 2 per cent of Australia's gross domestic product,[2] access to new agricultural export markets is central to our trade negotiations, and especially when the National Party provides the trade minister, as it usually does when the Coalition is in power. Other industries are barely mentioned.

But while National Party trade ministers are fiercely opposed to free trade in bananas and chicken, they have been far less concerned about protections for the manu-facturing industries. There aren't a lot of factories in National Party electorates.

Despite making Australian access to the US sugar market a line-in-the-sand issue, even John Howard's 'spe-cial' relationship with George W. Bush wasn't enough to get the United States to agree to something that would harm its heavily protected sugar industry. Like most lines in the sand, Howard's was washed away by the tide of po-litical power, and Australia signed a free-trade agreement with the United States that specifically prevented free trade in sugar. Needless to say, the US sugar industry has remained largely untouched by the twenty free-trade agreements the US government has entered into. It's the same story with the Japanese rice industry, which has been largely unaffected by its government's equally strong commitment to 'free trade'.

The recent Trans-Pacific Partnership (TPP), which its boosters described as an historically broad free-trade agreement, had little impact on the protections afforded to powerful interests in powerful countries. One analyst summarised the deal in the following terms:

> Japan budged little on rice, the U.S. gave few concessions on sugar and Canada's dairy system stayed intact in the Trans-Pacific Partnership agreement reached by trade ministers of 12 nations Monday, with the toughest agriculture issues resolved by tinkering.[3]

3. Free-trade agreements are about geopolitics.

Free-trade agreements provide a forum in which countries can demonstrate their friendship with (or fealty to) other countries. As the Productivity Commission has observed, 'the characterisation of security and strategic relationships as a central justification for a trade agreement is a cause of some concern, as the practical value of any contribution made by [bilateral and regional trade agreements] to such relationships is often not clear and yet such considerations can seem to dominate other considerations'.

Australian governments, for example, have given Chinese companies the right to bring their own labour, and Chinese wages and conditions, to Australia as they mine our resources and build our infrastructure.[4] Similarly, we have given US companies the right to appeal changes to our laws in international tribunals.[5]

Put simply, modern trade agreements typically require small countries to give up some of their sovereign rights. Evidently, those who have negotiated such deals on our behalf agree that the price we pay is worth it – but if they hold that view so strongly, then why are they so determined to characterise the decisions they make as a choice between 'free trade' and 'protection', rather than between independence and interdependence?

HOW TO CALL OUT THE ECONOBABBLE ABOUT FREE TRADE

Barnaby Joyce doesn't want free trade in bananas, John Howard never wanted free trade in guns, and even Cory Bernardi opposes free trade in drugs. Are there any in the current Coalition government who are committed to the freedom of people to move around the world chasing higher wages in the way the economic models assume?

The only way to win a debate about what the shock-jocks call 'free trade' is to make it clear to everyone that there is no such thing in its absolute form, and that conservative governments have no interest in achieving it. Only after it has been established that every industry and every political party supports the restrictions on trade that they like do you have any chance of winning a debate about the particular restrictions on trade that you prefer.

Democratic countries must make a wide range of judgements about what they think is in their national interest. There are benefits to encouraging trade and there are benefits to restricting trade. Reducing tariffs, quotas and other trade restrictions can drive innovation and efficiency, or it can make it more attractive for companies to shift work offshore to factories where workers are handcuffed to their sewing machines. Removing import restrictions on food can give Australian access to new and cheaper forms of fresh food, or it can allow new diseases to decimate our crops and result in Australians eating berries that have been watered with untreated sewerage.

Neither side of politics makes judgements like these perfectly all of the time, but few Australians even know that such decisions are being made. The extreme language of 'free trade' versus 'protection' conceals the significance of the wide range of decisions that would best be made with a high degree of public and parliamentary scrutiny.

What is really required is a rigorous, and inevitably messy, political debate about which kinds of protections we want to provide to which kinds of industries. But as long as we are having phoney debates about whether free trade is 'good' or 'bad', we can't start the hard discussions about better and worse forms of protection and deregulation.

THE TRUTH COMES OUT

In July 2015 the trade minister, Andrew Robb, made a

surprising admission, when it was put to him that the negotiations for the TPP lacked transparency:

> It's been a bit of a straw man, this issue of confidentiality. We've had over one thousand consultations. There are a range of industry groups at these negotiations, who we talk with every day, as has been the case with every time I've been to any negotiation anywhere in the world. The industry groups are there. It's quite a misnomer to suggest that we haven't contacted or we don't know what people want.[6]

In order to form his position, the minister had over a thousand consultations with industry groups. While unions, environmental groups and academics were prevented from seeing the draft text of the TPP deal, industry groups – the very same groups which publicly call for 'deregulation' and 'free trade' – were given privileged access to the negotiation process.

Two days later, Andrew Robb took up the point again: 'The industry groups from every country, including our own, make some often very ambitious claims. Those that are trying to defend their markets get fairly bullish about it, but this is the whole point of these agreements.'[7]

So there you have it. The 'whole point' of free-trade agreements is so industry groups can defend the regulations that make them money.

CHAPTER 7
THE USE AND ABUSE OF ECONOMIC MODELLING

E very time you hear a politician or business leader talk about the 4734 jobs that will be lost if we protect the environment, or the $4.673 billion 'cost to the economy' associated with an attempt to protect consumers, you are hearing the result of an economic model, and you should be sceptical. Very sceptical.

While the preceding chapters have considered specific arguments about specific issues, this chapter looks at the use and abuse of a particularly powerful tactic in the econobabblers' repertoire – the use and abuse of economic modelling.

An economic model is to the economy what a slot car is to a race car. The parts might look similar, but in reality they are totally different things. Joseph Stiglitz once made this very point. 'When I began the study of economics some forty-one years ago,' he said, 'I was struck by the incongruity between the models that I was taught and the world that I had seen growing up.'[1]

While economic modelling has become omnipresent in our public and political debate over the last fifteen years, it is almost entirely invisible in undergraduate economic degrees. Indeed, it is absent from most postgraduate economic studies. Most economists know as much about how the most widely used economic models work as most politicians – and by that I mean virtually nothing.

That doesn't mean that most economists are stupid; it means that economic modelling is something that almost no one understands. Of course, the fact that virtually no one knows what is going on inside the economic models that drive so much of our economic debate makes it the most powerful dialect of the language that is econobabble. What could silence the masses better than a language that only a handful of Australians speak?

Bizarrely, while the transparent and evidence-based modelling conducted by climate scientists has been widely criticised by those who profit from causing climate change, the top-secret and assumption-based economic modelling sold by a handful of economic consulting businesses in Australia is typically accepted uncritically by journalists, bureaucrats and senior politicians as objective truth.

The problem with most of the economic modelling used in public debate is that it is complete rubbish. The old adage in any form of modelling is 'garbage in, garbage out'. And while good modellers in most disciplines are quite open and transparent about the assumptions they make, most modelling in economics is conducted on the basis that the assumptions are 'commercial-in-confidence'. Indeed, a debate about the impact of increasing the GST reached a state of high farce in July 2015 when the lobby group Chartered Accountants Australia New Zealand 're-leased' economic modelling which 'showed' that increasing the GST to 15 per cent would collect an additional $256 billion.[2] The reason that the words *released* and *showed* need to be placed in quote marks is that not only did the accountants refuse to detail the assumptions on which their modelling was based, they also refused to release either the results or the name of the firm that conducted the economic modelling! They claimed that all these highly relevant details were 'commercial-in-confidence', despite the fact that they gave the headline results of their modelling to a journalist from the *Sydney Morning Herald*, which splashed them all over its front page.

Although not all modelling reports are as dodgy as that 'released' by Chartered Accountants Australia New Zealand, it's often the case that when you examine the technical appendices in the fat modelling reports – or, better yet, when you can question the modellers under oath in a court of law – the results can be as amusing as they are alarming. Consider the following admissions made by economic modellers when questioned under oath:

- The economist for Adani's Carmichael mine admitted that his model assumed that building an enormous new coal mine would not increase coal supply.[3]

- The economist for Yancoal's Ashton mine said that building new mines was 'not about jobs' and that this mine could increase retail wages.[4]

WHAT IS AN ECONOMIC MODEL?

For many people, economic modelling has become fundamental to 'serious policy debate'. People armed with economic modelling are often taken more seriously than those with twenty years' experience working on the same problem. The modelling result that suggests tens of thousands of jobs will be lost or created often trumps logic or experience that suggests such claims are nonsensical.

A model is a simplified representation of a more complex mechanism – and this is true of both slot cars and economics. A model is typically smaller, simpler and easier to build than the full-scale item. A model's main purpose is to illustrate the main features of the reality that it seeks to represent.

An economic model, of course, is not a physical thing like a model car. Rather, it is a mathematical representation of the linkages between the parts of the economy the modeller thinks are important. For example, an economic model of the link between economic growth and taxation would usually be based on historical data. A simple model might distinguish between the impact on economic growth of income tax, the GST and company profits tax, whereas a more complex model might distinguish between different types of economic growth (such as growth in exports, growth in consumer spending, growth in business investment) on a wider range of Commonwealth taxes, perhaps including capital gains tax, mining taxes and the fringe benefits tax.

Given that no model will ever be a perfectly accurate predictor, and that no model will cope well with unexpected events like the global financial crisis, the design of the models used by different organisations is determined by the use to which they are put. For example, a model designed to shed light on the budget deficit or surplus for the following year will likely have less detail but a greater capacity to predict the budget result than a model designed by an investment firm to estimate the amount of tax likely to be paid by individual mining companies.

Put simply, no model can capture the complexity of the entire Australian economy. No model can accurately predict the economic impact of something that has never happened before. And no model is free from a large number of assumptions, which, in reality, are often little more than somebody's best guess.

Honest modellers are humble about what their model can and can't do. They are transparent about the assumptions they have made, and they present their results in a way that minimises the chance that they will be misinterpreted.

Well-paid modellers, on the other hand, make bold claims about what their model can do. They use higher-order econobabble to discourage most economists from pressing them very hard about the assumptions they have made and, when pushed, they simply refuse to reveal them.

If science is the process of allowing others to test your hypothesis by following the same steps you have taken, then there is nothing scientific about most commercial economic modelling in Australia.

TRUST ME, I'M AN ECONOMIC MODELLER

The economic modeller's best trick is to imply accuracy by using precision. When someone states that a carbon price will cause the mining industry to lose precisely 23,510 jobs, we don't imagine they could be bluffing. But they are.

In reality, economic modellers use this combination of highly precise predictions and a refusal to explain how their models work to create a mystique around their work: mere mortals fear to question them, let alone lampoon their results. The scientists doing climate modelling should take a closer look at what the economists are getting away with.

Thanks to economic modelling, we know, for instance, that the Melbourne Grand Prix generates tens of millions of dollars' worth of 'economic benefits'. (Of course, we ignore the costs of the noise pollution it generates and the inconvenience it causes Melbourne's residents.) We also know that causing climate change and allowing duck hunting will 'create jobs'.

Buried in all such results are assumptions about the value of your time, the value of peace and quiet or the value of the natural environment (usually zero – but that's an assumption). Such assumptions are of course highly significant, yet those spruiking the models are rarely, if ever, asked about them.

It's even possible to put a value on a human life. People often think that it's difficult, if not impossible, to do this, but in fact it's easy. The hard part is putting an *accurate* value on human life, but if you write enough reports that are sufficiently hard to understand, no one will ask you a simple question like: 'How on earth did you value the life of a child?'

In 2008 a Department of Finance report entitled 'Establishing a Monetary Value for Lives Saved: Issues and Controversies' valued an Australian human life at $151,000 per year.[5] That said, individual departments, consultants and lobbyists are free to use their own assumptions. Of course, citizens are also free to pore over the modellers' thick reports looking for such assumptions, but few do. You might argue that it is the public, or its representatives in parliament, who should weigh up such 'life and death' matters. But while the Australian parliament has held inquiries into everything from the effectiveness of beef marketing to whether wind turbines cause 'wind turbine syndrome', no Australian parliament has ever held an inquiry into the value of a human life, as used when making policy decisions.

While the United States has never held such an inquiry either, Congress has made it clear how it does *not* want human life to be valued. Back in 2003 the US Environmental Protection Agency (EPA) flirted with changing the way it valued human life, in order to recognise the fact that many economists think the life of an old and sick person is not worth as much as the life of a young and healthy person.[6] The flirting didn't last long. Here's what happened.

Until the early 2000s the EPA had valued all American lives equally when conducting so-called cost–benefit analyses of policy changes. Then it began experimenting with discounting the value of some lives. Given that air pollution generally kills the old and the sick, the consequences of devaluing the lives of the elderly were highly significant. By assuming that the old and the sick weren't worth as much as an average American, it became harder to show that the benefits to the population of tougher air-pollution regulations were greater than the cost of tougher regulation of the car companies. Put simply, the EPA's 'pensioner discount' assumption could have saved air polluters a lot of money.

Not surprisingly, once the public realised that economists were devaluing their grandmothers' lives, they got interested. Congress eventually passed a bill banning federal government funding for research that discounted the value of retirees' lives.

While the veil of econobabble was in place and the debate focused on 'cost–benefit analyses', 'discount rates' and 'morbidity rates', US citizens were happy to leave 'life and death' issues to the economists and their models. But when the econobabble was stripped away and the public caught a glimpse of the way in which economists were making their decisions, things changed quickly.

ECONOMISTS KNOW THE PRICE OF EVERYTHING AND THE VALUE OF NOTHING

Economists have a wide range of techniques for attempting to value goods and services that are not bought and sold in markets. These techniques allow economists to *estimate* the 'value' of fresh air or clean water, or of protecting an endangered species or mitigating climate change.

While all such estimates are based on a wide range of assumptions – many of which non-economists find highly implausible – it is important to note that economists don't even know how to accurately value a house, a car, a bottle of water or a song. Economists, like philosophers before them, have spent centuries arguing about what *value* is and how to measure it. Is the value of something based on its usefulness, its necessity, its scarcity or the amount of effort that went into its construction?

Consider this: if we can't live without water, and if we have no real *need* for diamonds, why are diamonds so much more valuable than water? If your answer is that scarcity determines value, then why aren't endangered species worth spending a fortune to protect?

Some people think that goods are more 'real', and thus more 'valuable', than services. Such thinking implies that making musical instruments generates more value than playing them. But if playing an instrument isn't valuable, then what's the point in making them?

People sometimes think that the *price* of something is the same as its *value*. But if that's the case, then how can identical things have different values? As we saw in an earlier chapter, it costs an Australian more to download a song from iTunes than it costs a US citizen – is the song inherently worth more in Australia?

After hundreds of years arguing about what value really means, most economists from the 1950s onwards made a strategic decision to simply work on the assumption that price and value were one and the same thing. While this assumption made no philosophical sense, it did make it much easier for economists to conduct analysis of the enormous quantity of price data floating around.

In more recent decades, however, economists have moved well past any nagging doubts that price and value might not be the same thing, and now assume that we can place a value on human life, human pain and suffering, species extinction and global climate change by asking people how much they would be 'willing and able to pay' to avoid a particular outcome.

The ethical consequences of assuming that the life of a rich person is worth far more than the life of a poor person (because a rich person would be 'willing and able to pay' more for life-lengthening services) are neatly summarised in a memo written by the former chief economist of the World Bank, Lawrence Summers. While the 'Summers Memo', as it is now known, is claimed by its author to have been 'sarcastic', a close reading and a little translation provides a window onto the values and the fundamental limitations of economic modelling.

The Summers Memo

'Dirty' Industries: Just between you and me, shouldn't the World Bank be encouraging MORE migration of the dirty industries to the LDCs [Least Developed Countries]? I can think of three reasons:

The measurements of the costs of health impairing pollution depends on the foregone earnings from increased morbidity and mortality. From this point of view a given amount of health impairing pollution should be done in the country with the lowest cost, which will be the country with the lowest wages. I think the economic logic behind dumping a load of toxic waste in the lowest wage country is impeccable and we should face up to that.

Translation: we value human life based on lost earnings. From this point of view, pollution should occur in poor countries, as the people it kills there are worth less than people in rich countries.

> The costs of pollution are likely to be non-linear as the initial increments of pollution probably have very low cost. I've always thought that under-populated countries in Africa are vastly UNDER-polluted, their air quality is probably vastly inefficiently low compared to Los Angeles or Mexico City. Only the lamentable facts that so much pollution is generated by non-tradable industries (transport, electrical generation) and that the unit transport costs of solid waste are so high prevent world welfare enhancing trade in air pollution and waste.

Translation: Just as a drop of hot water won't harm you but a cup of hot water can burn you badly, the amount of harm pollution does rises faster than the 'dose' of pollution to which a person is exposed. I've always thought that under-populated countries in Africa are vastly under-polluted, and that they don't have enough pollution compared with Los Angeles or Mexico City. It's a pity that so much air pollution is caused by industries such as transport and electricity generation, because otherwise we would be able to make the world a better place by shifting a lot of the polluting activities to the under-polluted developing countries that have low-value human lives.

The demand for a clean environment for aesthetic and
health reasons is likely to have very high income
elasticity. The concern over an agent that causes a one in
a million change in the odds of prostrate[sic] cancer is
obviously going to be much higher in a country where
people survive to get prostrate[sic] cancer than in a
country where under 5 mortality is 200 per thousand.
Also, much of the concern over industrial atmosphere
discharge is about visibility impairing particulates. These
discharges may have very little direct health impact.
Clearly trade in goods that embody aesthetic pollution
concerns could be welfare enhancing. While production
is mobile the consumption of pretty air is a non-tradable.

Translation: Rich people would be willing to pay a lot
more money for a healthy and attractive physical environment. Indeed, poor people who are likely to die young
from preventable disease probably won't even live long
enough to get the cancers caused by many pollutants, so
we might as well pollute them anyway. Also, a lot of the
concern about particulate pollution is for aesthetic rather
than health reasons. It would be great if rich people could
pay to move the unattractive pollution to a poor country,
because you can produce pollution anywhere but you can
only enjoy pretty air where you are right now.

The problem with the arguments against all of these
proposals for more pollution in LDCs (intrinsic rights

> to certain goods, moral reasons, social concerns, lack
> of adequate markets, etc.) could be turned around and
> used more or less effectively against every Bank
> proposal for liberalization.

Translation: the World Bank has been making decisions that are good for rich people and bad for poor people since we were set up.

Of course, the fact economists can plug 'GDP per capita' or 'average wages' into their models as a proxy for the value of human life doesn't mean they should. By definition, when a country experiences a recession its GDP falls, and so therefore does its GDP per capita. Did American lives become less valuable during the global financial crisis?

And remember that GDP only captures 'market production' and ignores 'household production'. For example, a parent providing childcare to their own child contributes nothing to GDP, while a parent who pays someone else to care for their child increases GDP. Are the lives of people who care for their own children worth less than those who pay others to do it?

About ten years ago, a lawyer rang me to ask if I would do some (economic) modelling. 'It depends,' I said. 'What's the job?'

'We want you to put a dollar value on the life of a dead mother,' said the lawyer. 'We are suing a doctor for medical negligence, and the insurance company wants to value her life at zero because she wasn't working. She had no future earning potential. Can you estimate the value of the housework she would have performed?'

I still feel sad when I think about it: for the family, for myself, and for a society in which asking such a question is not only acceptable but also necessary. The dilemma for the widower and the lawyer, and for me, was that if someone didn't put a dollar value on the love and care that a mother gives her children, the father would wind up with even less money to care for the kids he would be bringing up by himself.

Of course, economists have no real way to value love and affection, so I valued ironing, laundry and childcare instead. I got my hands on data about how mothers with three kids use their time. I found data on the price of buying individual household services like ironing, and the price of live-in maids and nannies. I forecast the age at which the kids would leave home. My forecast was based on a meaningless average of kids who do go to uni and kids who don't. My spreadsheets were huge, complex, scrupulously referenced and entirely meaningless. Like all good forecasters, I estimated the 'value' of the dead woman's life to the cent, and as happens in all good negotiations, the lawyers ultimately settled for a nice round number. The only good thing about the number was that it was bigger than zero.

This applies at a societal level too. One of the major benefits of tackling climate change is that a lot of lives will be saved. But what are those lives worth? When politicians and economists say that the costs of tackling climate change are greater than the benefits of doing so, they are not making a statement about the economy; they are making a statement about the value of human lives.

Democracies have to find ways to make hard decisions, such as:

- Should we pay more tax and have higher-quality health services?

- Should the government subsidise expensive new drugs, even if they only lengthen the lives of those suffering from rare illnesses for a few months?

- Should seeing a doctor when we feel sick be free to the patient, or should the 'user' pay?

- Should we tackle climate change, or should we just see how things pan out?

Different people, and different countries, have entirely different views about such questions. While the answers have financial and economic consequences, the questions are fundamentally ethical ones. It is a sad fact that the main purpose of economic modelling in Australian public debate is to conceal the ethical dimension of significant policy questions. Having been well paid to make assumptions about the value of human life, the value of avoiding illness and the future value of increased investment in education, many economic modellers now refuse to reveal what those assumptions are, preferring only to focus on the 'answers' their models generate.

If you could bring yourself to read economic modelling reports carefully, you'd be rewarded with some good laughs. For example, you would discover that the economic modelling used to predict the impact of the carbon price on the Australian economy assumed that, as the carbon price rose, the volume of farts per sheep per year would decline.[7]

It isn't too much to say that almost no one outside the companies selling such nonsense to governments knows about the assumptions on which the models are built. That is why the models are so powerful! Garbage in, garbage out.

CONCLUSION

When done well, economic modelling can provide insights into the more and less obvious linkages between a change to one part of the economy and the impact in other parts of the economy. When used cautiously by informed adults who understand the limitations of what they are doing, modelling can be perceptive and illuminating.

Or it can be used to dress up self-interest as the national interest. When well-paid economic modellers team up with the PR industry on behalf of lobby groups with lots of money, economic models can unleash a flood of econobabble – nonsense that is incomprehensible to most economists, let alone to most voters.

While such a torrent might be impossible to stop, it can be diverted. Journalists, and indeed all citizens, should be asking some simple questions about the economic models used by politicians and lobbyists, and they should demand simple answers in response. If the person spruiking the modelling can't or won't answer a simple question about their assumptions, then either they don't know what they're talking about or they are trying to deceive you – it's as simple as that.

CHAPTER 8
WHAT CAN BE DONE?

Democracies use words, not guns, to resolve disputes. And econobabble can be a powerful weapon. In the public contest of ideas, words can illuminate and lead to improvements in our lives, or they can insult our intelligence, silence citizens, limit the menu of policy options we can consider and fundamentally harm our democracy.

The wall of sound made by the econobabblers drowns out genuine conversation. It creates a cloak, behind which the real objectives of those with powerful voices can hide. Put simply, econobabble helps powerful groups hide the fact that they are getting what they want. Honest economics can help society understand the choices and trade-offs we face, but econobabble conceals most options and disparages most of those that remain. It is central to convincing the public that 'there is no alternative'.

The idea that 'the markets will punish us' if we pursue the social and environmental goals that a majority of Australians want has destroyed much of the ambition in our nation's political debate. But it is not just progressive political parties that self-censor in order to avoid the ridicule of those who 'understand what the market needs'. Unions, non-government organisations, think-tanks and individuals often embrace the language of their oppressors, and in so doing reinforce the belief that 'everyone knows' that 'we can't afford' to provide the level of services that we could afford to provide a generation ago, when our GDP was much smaller.

This book rests on two main premises. The first is that there are no good economic reasons that Australia cannot collect more tax revenue and spend that money on health, education and community services, or use regulation to ensure that 'market outcomes' do not come at the expense of our values, our vision for the future, or the natural environment.

The second premise, which perhaps is more important, is that a significant number of Australians aspire to live in such a society. History tells us that it is possible for a small country to develop innovative social policies that have never been tried elsewhere. And international observation tells us that a wide range of countries with lower levels of national income than ours have succeeded in providing far higher levels of health, education, housing and transport services to their citizens than we do. If we want a different country, we can certainly afford it.

But despite the overwhelming public support for closing tax loopholes and spending the money saved on better health and education, it doesn't happen. This is clearly not a failure to sell 'a vision'; it is a failure to convince people that we can pursue that vision without 'wrecking the economy' or 'making the markets angry'.

There is no need to run a PR campaign about the benefits of investing in health, education or the protection of the environment – the public are already convinced. The problem is not a lack of support for 'the product'; it is the ability of the econobabblers to exaggerate 'the price'.

So what should those who want a better country do, if they want to win a debate with the econobabblers, and with the rest of their fellow Australians, about the desirability and the affordability of the society they want? Let's start with the don'ts.

1. Don't accept the premise that we can't afford a better society – they don't.

Australians are, on average, among the richest people ever to live on the earth. While poverty exists in Australia, collectively we control sufficient resources that we can solve any problem we wish to solve. Of course, we can't afford to solve *every* problem that we want. Choosing which problems to solve and which problems to ignore is where democracy, public debate and econobabble come into their own.

Saying that we 'can't afford' to do something sounds a lot nicer than saying that we 'don't want' to do it. Imagine if a prime minster said, 'I don't want to improve the quality of aged care. I'd rather provide tax cuts to high-income earners.' Of course, it'd be much easier and less controversial (if dishonest) for the PM to say, 'We need to cut taxes in order to provide an incentive for people to work hard, so that in the future, once we get the budget under control, we can responsibly invest in higher-quality aged-care services.' Econobabble helps conceal that such a prime minister is making a choice about which group is favoured first.

Those who want to invest more in public services must never accept the premise that the Australian government cannot afford to do something. Conservatives never do. They never argue that money spent on fighter jets, or on saving the details of every phone call you make or email you send, is 'unsustainable' or 'unaffordable'. Those words are reserved for the things they don't want to spend money on – like the aged pension.

2. Don't accept their stated goal of maximising economic growth – they don't.

Conservatives always say that the goal of their policies is 'economic growth' for Australia. But economic growth is a means to an end, not an end in itself. Economic growth is usually measured as the rate of growth in gross domestic product (GDP), which really just means the amount of stuff that was bought and sold in a given year. GDP is an important indicator, especially if you want to know about the volume of stuff being produced, but the idea that simply increasing GDP should be our major objective is so silly that not even the conservatives believe it.

Virtually every economist would argue that investing in high-quality education is a great way to increase economic growth in the long run, yet virtually every conservative government wants to cut spending on public education. If they were serious about increasing GDP, then conservatives would be enthusiastic about investing in education for the entire population. But they aren't, so they don't. What they are serious about is cutting public spending, so that they can cut taxes for the rich.

Similarly, if conservatives truly wanted to increase GDP, then they would be keen to provide low-cost, high-quality childcare to parents who wanted to re-enter the labour force after having a child. There is no more effective way of increasing the proportion of the population in work than to help young parents re-enter the labour market when they are ready to. As with most problems, however, conservatives prefer to argue that offering tax cuts to high-income earners who already work is a better way to stimulate labour force participation than providing the kind of widespread free child care provided in France.[1]

Progressives are often so busy pointing out (quite rightly) that GDP is not the 'be-all and end-all' that they don't notice that conservatives actually agree with them. By pretending to care about GDP, conservative econobabblers can say things like: 'We need tax reform to provide incentives that will kick-start the economy.' What they really mean is: 'I'd like to cut taxes for the wealthy instead of helping get more parents back into the labour force.' Econobabble is much more polite than the truth.

3. Don't fall for false choices – they were invented to make your life a misery.

If you had three kids who were slipping off a cliff and only two hands to grab them with, which of your children would you let die? Kids love asking parents questions like that, and most parents find a way of refusing to answer. It's easy to think up some political questions that most people can't or won't answer:

- Should we spend more money on sick kids or on improving the lives of the elderly?

- Should we invest in new schools or new hospitals?

- Should we protect old-growth forests or throw forestry workers on the scrapheap?

- Should we tackle climate change or help lift people in India out of poverty by giving them access to 'cheap electricity'?

Creating a phoney dilemma is the central political strategy of the modern conservative. It works because progressives often care about helping people *and* about protecting the environment. Making progressives 'choose' between which vulnerable groups to help, or between helping people and protecting the environment, diminishes the enthusiasm of the individuals fighting for simple causes, as well as making it harder for organisations (such as unions and environmental groups) to work together. Conservatives rarely get caught up in dilemmas about which group to help; their default position is to cut taxes as much as possible and let everyone who isn't rich look after themselves.

The only effective way to response to a false dilemma is to reject the premise that we can't afford to help multiple groups. We don't have to make such choices if we collect more tax revenue, and we can do that by closing the loopholes that help only the rich. Similarly, progressives must flatly reject the premise that the best way to create jobs is to destroy the environment. The data is quite clear that investment in health and education leads to employment of far more people than investment in mining or forestry.

4. Don't use their objectives to validate your own.
Conservatives don't really prioritise reducing the budget deficit. If they did, then they would be happy to close the tax loopholes from which they benefit; the Treasury would collect tens of billions of dollars more per year in revenue. And, as we've seen, conservatives don't really think GDP growth is the nation's top priority. Given a choice between investments in education (which will enhance productivity) and defence spending (which won't), they will take defence spending any day.

Unfortunately, many progressive organisations have come to believe the econobabble, and have distorted their own language so that they fit in with the 'accepted wisdom'. This can result in community organisations accepting (and therefore validating) the existence of a 'budget emergency' and an 'ageing crisis', and accepting cuts to health services. Or it can result in environmental groups arguing that nature should be protected for its economic benefits. But neither of these topics should be decided by reference to economics alone.

The main reason we should spend more money on preventive health is that it helps people avoid needless pain and suffering. It is a good idea. It is wrong to withhold treatment from vulnerable groups when we know the long-term consequences of this. The fact that well-designed preventive health measures can save our nation a lot of money down the track is a bonus – it's not the main reason we should invest in them. Should parents only vaccinate their kids if the cost of the vaccination is lower than the cost of treating the illness? Or do most parents want to spare their kids unnecessary pain and suffering?

Similarly, the main reason we should protect old-growth forests from clear-felling is that once such eco-systems are destroyed, we will never see their like again. In Tasmania today there is logging proposed in one of the last known nesting sites of the endangered swift parrot. Once it's extinct, we will never see it again. Those who want to protect these remaining wild places because they think it is right to do so, and because they want their kids and their grandkids to have the chance to see them, should say so boldly. The fact that tourism creates far more jobs than the forestry industry (7 per cent of Tasmania's jobs are in tourism, versus less than 1 per cent in forestry) is a bonus, but it should never be the central argument.[2] If the world price of woodchips soared and tourists decided that casinos were more fun to visit than grand forests, should environmentalists abandon their efforts to save the forests?

The economic arguments for good social and environmental policy should only ever play a supporting role in how we advocate for them. To do otherwise accepts the false premise that the GDP growth and budget surpluses should be our ultimate goal, and leaves the advocates vulnerable whenever market prices shift.

5. Don't stay out of economic debates – they matter.

Perhaps the biggest mistake made by many progressives is to stay out of the economic debate on the basis that 'economics is crap' or that it's a mistake to 'engage in their frame'. Whatever the reason, the consequence of staying out of major debates about 'the budget' and 'the economy' is that it cedes to the econobabblers the high ground of Australian public debate.

Conservatives rarely deign to debate the specifics of why we shouldn't have a childcare system as good as France's, a public health system as good as England's or a public transport system as good as New York's. Why bother with actual debate when you can simply argue that 'we can't afford it'?

The idea that progressives can't win when they are talking about the economy has no basis in Australian history. During Labor's longest post-war stint in office, the Hawke and Keating governments drove, and dominated, the national economic debate.

Budgets spell out a government's priorities, and these reflect a society's priorities. It is inconceivable that progressives can reshape our nation without reshaping Commonwealth and state budgets. Similarly, government policies drive the shape of economic growth. While much is made by progressives of the limitations of economic growth as an indicator of progress, it is hard to imagine an environmental group that is indifferent to the question of whether we should be building more coal mines or more wind turbines. Similarly, it is hard to imagine a health group that is indifferent to the question of whether we should be investing more in roads or in hospitals. The simplistic debate about whether economic growth is 'good' or 'bad' prevents progressives from engaging in a genuine conversation about which parts of the economy they want to grow, and which parts they want to decline.

Enough with the don'ts. What should those who are sick of having their public debate starved of oxygen by the econobabblers actually do?

1. Do call out the bullshit every time you hear it.
You can't influence a debate unless you're in it. Yelling at the television, moaning to your friends, convincing yourself that no one pays attention to the 'mainstream media' or having a phone hook-up with aggrieved folk from other NGOs does nothing to counter the lies told by the econobabblers or to shift the debate. Debates can only ever be won by those who participate in them.

It's true that no one person, or no one organisation, can

successfully break through the wall of sound created by the econobabblers. But when climate sceptics use that argument to justify inaction on climate change, most progressives become livid. Yes, an individual has little power to reshape a national debate – but tens of thousands of determined people definitely can.

You (and anyone else) can ...

- Phone a radio station to call out BS when you hear it.

- Write a letter to the editor of a newspaper.

- Post a polite but mocking tweet or Facebook message to inform and empower your friends (#econobabble).

- Write to individual politicians and businesspeople to let them know that you see through the absurdity of their comments.

And of course you can encourage your friends to do the same. Organisations and community groups also can do all of the above. As well, they can ...

- Organise events to inform their members about the need to take on the econobabblers and the benefits of doing so.

- Change the way they communicate to ensure that they aren't inadvertently reinforcing the power of econobabble.

- Organise, or participate in, public debates about important economic issues.

2. Do sell the big picture by selling the small picture, and sell the small picture by selling the big picture.

The world changes all the time. Our world today barely resembles the world of 100 years ago. And there is no doubt that the world in 100 years' time will be fundamentally different again. The only thing that is certain is that, by then, the politicians, policies and politics of today will all have been washed away.

Given that the world will change, and change radically, all democratic fights are really fights about the direction and pace of *change*. This should provide a big advantage to progressives, who should want change, because of course conservatives should want to leave things as they are. But it doesn't provide that advantage, partly because these days the words *progressive* and *conservative* are more like team names than statements of philosophy. Progressives often want to conserve things (usually elements of the natural environment), while conservatives usually want to change things (especially in relation to the nature of work and, bizarrely, the world's climate).

But philosophical labels aside, there is no doubt that many progressives get confused about whether they should be fighting 'big battles', like tackling world poverty, or 'small problems', like building community resilience and encouraging street gardening. This is, of course, a phoney dilemma.

The world is changed not by global consensus but by the pressure of actions at a range of levels. If absolutely everyone stopped hunting rhinos, all rhinos would be safe from hunting. But what if we can't get everyone to agree to that? Well, if enough individuals declare their hostility to rhino hunting, it becomes politically possible to ban it. Individual actions help deliver political actions. The fossil-fuel divestment campaign is powerful for exactly this reason.

Individuals campaigning for better funding for their local school can simultaneously use their local campaign to raise awareness about the need for governments to invest more in all schools. National organisations calling for greater Commonwealth funding for all schools can simultaneously call for a better tax system that enables government to improve the quality of all public services. Specific examples help sell general propositions, and general propositions help explain the importance of individual changes. It's not either/or – it's both.

3. Do take the high ground and engage in debates.

Anyone who is serious about achieving a significant increase in public investment in health, education or public transport needs to be just as serious about the bigger-picture issues of tax policy, fiscal policy and economic management. Just as *MasterChef* contestants who are 'passionate about their food' but uninterested in the realities of running a small business are unlikely to serve many customers in the long run, so progressives who are passionate about improving the health system but bored by talk of budgets are unlikely to achieve significant change.

People who care deeply about spending need to care

deeply about revenue too. Conservative econobabblers rarely argue that money spent on the sick or on school kids is 'wasted'. They simply argue that 'we can't afford it'. The Right does not run campaigns to convince the public that we should spend less on public schools; they campaign to cut taxes, knowing that the less we collect in tax, the less we will spend on schools.

Similarly, groups that want to win fights about workplace or environmental protection laws need to be engaged in bigger-picture debates about the role of regulation in general. Just as those from the Right use general fights about tax to win specific fights about spending, they also use big-picture fights about 'red tape' and 'nanny states' to win specific fights about particular industrial relations or environmental regulations.

If progressive organisations stay out of 'theoretical' or 'ideological' battles about the role of regulation in society, they cede the high ground. When it comes time to push for, or protect, a specific regulation, they have to fight uphill. And the lesson of the last twenty years is that they usually lose.

4. Do work with others outside your 'silo' – you are not always your own best spokesperson.

Many individuals and organisations have no interest in participating in debates about which they are not 'passionate', even if they generally support the cause. Fair enough. They don't have to engage in the debate personally – they can empower others to do so on their behalf.

Business groups often organise in such a way that individual companies are spared the effort, or indeed the embarrassment, of calling for the major reforms they want. For example, the Business Council of Australia has waged a twenty-year battle, on behalf of its members, to lower the company tax rate and lower the minimum wage. Such an approach spares individual company CEOs, who often earn millions of dollars per year, from having to argue that their low-paid workers should earn even less.

If individual NGOs and unions can't or don't want to take on groups like the BCA, then they need to create or support groups that will. Groups that want to see an increase in public funding for Indigenous health might feel they have little in common with groups that advocate for young people with disabilities. In reality, both lose out when the BCA achieves further cuts in the corporate tax rate, and both would benefit from an overarching campaign to collect more revenue.

But just as the CEO of a big company can leave the battle to lower their workers' wages to their delegate at the BCA, so too can the leaders of diverse community groups leave the details of specific tax debates to others, if they wish.

5. Do use new ideas to build new alliances.
It is often easier to get people to unite around a new idea than to change their minds about an old idea. Unfortunately for progressives, the flood of econobabble that dominates our public debate makes it difficult for new

ideas to be taken seriously. Journalists, politicians and even other progressives are often quick to ask what sound like important questions:

- How will this be paid for?

- Have you done any modelling?

- Isn't it better to let the market solve problems like that?

- Haven't people tried to solve this problem and failed before?

Of course policy ideas should be carefully scrutinised, but it is banal to dismiss new ideas on the basis that one of the world's richest countries 'can't afford it' or because a certain ideology insists problems that markets can't solve aren't worth solving.

A FINAL WORD

Those who want to change the world for the better by improving our social and environmental conditions are, at present, fighting an uphill battle against well-funded opponents. Econobabble is the first line of defence used by those resisting changes that are both popular and equitable.

Unfortunately, in the short term at least, those who want the world to notice their one good idea will first have to join the fight against the econobabblers. Until public debate once again takes place in plain English, the vast majority of Australians will continue to believe that 'the markets will be angry' unless we sacrifice the sick, the poor and the environment.

Managing the economy is important. Unemployment devastates lives. Budgets spell out priorities. Trade with other countries matters. The Australian public will only elect people who care about the economy, but you don't need to be an expert to ask simple questions about it. Whenever you hear a politician talking econobabble, just ask them to say it again in English.

If you have listened closely and sought clarification and you still don't understand, then the person moving their lips either doesn't understand or is trying to pull the wool over your eyes. So the next time you hear someone talking econobabble bullshit, call it out for what it is.

NOTES

CHAPTER 1: THE LANGUAGE OF DECEPTION

1. See, for example, *Per Capita Tax Survey 2015: Public attitudes towards taxation and public expenditure* (http://percapita.org.au/research/per-capita-tax-survey-2015).

2. See Daniel Hurst, 'Tony Abbott backs away from iron ore inquiry after lobbying by BHP and Rio', *The Guardian*, 19 May 2015 (www.theguardian.com/business/2015/may/19/tony-abbott-backs-away-from-iron-ore-inquiry-after-lobbying-by-bhp-and-rio).

CHAPTER 2: TACKLING CLIMATE CHANGE

1. Australian Bureau of Statistics (ABS), 'Labour Force, Australia, Detailed, Quarterly, Nov 2015', catalogue number 6291.0.55.003, 17 December 2015 (www.abs.gov.au/AUSSTATS/abs@.nsf/DetailsPage/6291.0.55.003Nov%202015?OpenDocument).

2. Laura Tingle, 'Malcolm Turnbull rejects coal ban as chief scientist talks zero emissions', *Australian Financial Review*, 27 October 2015 (www.afr.com/business/energy/malcolm-turnbull-rejects-coal-ban-as-chief-scientist-talks-zero-emissions-20151026-gkj8hi).

3. See, for example, Sarah-Jane Tasker, 'Ivan Glasenberg takes swipe

at Rio Tinto, says Glencore won't flood coal market', *The Australian*, 4 March 2015 (www.theaustralian.com.au/business/ mining-energy/ivan-glasenberg-takes-swipe-at-rio-tinto-says-glencore-wont-flood-coal-market/story-e6frg9df-1227247304912).

4. International Energy Agency, 2012, *CO2 Emissions from Fuel Combustion 2012*. Paris, Organisation for Economic Co-operation and Development.

5. Mick Peel, Roderick Campbell & Richard Denniss, 2014, *Mining the Age of Entitlement*. Canberra, The Australia Institute (www.tai.org.au/content/mining-age-entitlement).

6. Queensland Government (2013) *Queensland Treasury Response to Commonwealth Grants Commission: Response to terms of reference for Commonwealth Grants Commission 2015 Methodology Review* (www.cgc.gov.au/index. php?option=com_attachments&task=download&id=1728).

7. Peel, Campbell & Denniss, *Mining the Age of Entitlement*.

8. Peel, Campbell & Denniss, *Mining the Age of Entitlement*.

9. Bruce Chapman, 2011, 'How Many Jobs is 23,510, Really?', Crawford School Research Paper No. 4, Crawford School of Public Policy, Australian National University, Canberra (http:// papers.ssrn.com/sol3/papers.cfm?abstract_id=1873643).

10. See, for example, Cecilia Jamasmie, 'Glencore axes jobs, coal output at Australia's mine as price collapses', 7 December 2015 (www.mining.com/glencore-axes-jobs-coal-output-at-australias-mine-as-price-collapses).

11. ABS, 'Labour Force, Australia, Detailed, Quarterly, Aug 2015', 17 September 2015 (www.abs.gov.au/AUSSTATS/abs@.nsf/Look up/6291.0.55.003Main+Features1Aug%202015?OpenDocument).

12. 'FactCheck: Do the Liberals have "a secret plan" to axe 20,000 public service jobs?', *The Conversation*, 24 July 2013 (https:// theconversation.com/factcheck-do-the-liberals-have-a-secret-plan-to-axe-20-000-public-service-jobs-16032).

13. Cole Latimer, 'Mining Still Driving QLD Economy', *Australian Mining*, 13 December 2011 (www.australianmining. com.au/news/mining-still-driving-qld-economy).

14. ABS, 'Labour Force, Australia, Detailed, Quarterly, Aug 2015', 17 September 2015 (www.abs.gov.au/AUSSTATS/abs@.nsf/Look up/6291.0.55.003Main+Features1Aug%202015?OpenDocument).

15. See Lawrence Consulting, 2015, *Economic Impact of the Minerals and Energy Sector on the Queensland Economy 2014/15*, prepared for the Queensland Resources Council

(www.qrc.org.au/_dbase_upl/EconomicImpactofResources
SectorExecutive%20Summary.pdf); and ABS, 'Labour Force,
Australia, Detailed, Quarterly, Aug 2015', 17 September 2015
(www.abs.gov.au/AUSSTATS/abs@.nsf/Lookup/6291.0.55.003
Main+Features1Aug%202015?OpenDocument).

16. 'Is the Mining Industry the Largest Indigenous Employer?
Check the facts', *Facts Fight Back*, 16 July 2013 (www.
factsfightback.org.au/is-the-mining-industry-the-largest-
indigenous-employer-check-the-facts).

17. ABS, 'Labour Force, Australia, Detailed, Quarterly, Aug 2015',
17 September 2015 (www.abs.gov.au/AUSSTATS/abs@.nsf/Look
up/6291.0.55.003Main+Features1Aug%202015?OpenDocument).

18. Kathleen Donaghey & AAP, 'Premier Newman will not halt
port and industry development on Queensland's coast to
protect Great Barrier Reef', *The Sunday Mail*, 2 June 2012
(www.couriermail.com.au/news/queensland/premier-
campbell-newman-will-not-halt-port-and-industry-
development-on-queenslands-coast-to-protect-great-barrier-
reef/story-e6freoof-1226381294353).

19. See state and federal government budget papers, and Deloitte
Access Economics, 2014, *Estimated Company Tax, MRRT,
Carbon Tax and Royalties Expenses for the Minerals Sector:
Report prepared for the Minerals Council of Australia* (www.
minerals.org.au/file_upload/files/reports/DAE_-_MCA_
Royalty_and_company_tax_estimates_30_July_(1).pdf).

20. Tim Blair, 'Leader Followed', *The Telegraph*, 14 May 2012
(http://blogs.news.com.au/dailytelegraph/timblair/index.php/
dailytelegraph/comments/leader_followed).

21. ABS, 'Balance of Payments and International Investment
Position, Australia, Sep 2015', catalogue number 5302.0,
1 December 2015.

22. ABS, 'Balance of Payments and International Investment
Position, Australia, Sep 2015', catalogue number 5302.0,
1 December 2015.

23. Queensland Government Office of Economic and Statistical
Research, 2015, 'International visitors (a)(b) by Queensland
Tourism region, 2005–06 to 2014–15' (www.oesr.qld.gov.au/
regions/far-north/tables/internat-visitors-qld-tourism-region/
index.php).

24. Fidelis Rego and Rhianwen Whitney, 'Silver lining to mining
boom's farm impact', ABC News Online, 15 November 2012

(www.abc.net.au/news/2012-11-15/silver-lining-to-mining-booms-farm-impact/4373268).

25. Larry Schlesinger, 'Sydney hotels surge to best performance in 20 years', *Australian Financial Review*, 15 December 2015 (www.afr.com/real-estate/sydney-hotels-surge-to-best-performance-in-20-years-20151214-glnk7c).

26. See Independent Pricing & Regulatory Tribunal, www.ipart. nsw.gov.au/Home/About_Us/FAQs?dlv_FAQ%20List= (dd_Industries=electricity).

CHAPTER 3: WHAT REALLY CAUSES UNEMPLOYMENT?

1. Joe Hockey, *Budget Speech 2014–15*, 13 May 2014, Canberra, Australian Government (http://budget.gov.au/2014-15/content/speech/html/speech.htm).

2. Hockey, *Budget Speech 2014–15*.

3. Joseph Stiglitz, 'Australia, you don't know how good you've got it', *The Sydney Morning Herald*, 2 September 2013 (www.smh.com.au/comment/australia-you-dont-know-how-good-youve-got-it-20130901-2sytb.html).

4. Tony Abbott, 'Prime Minister – Address to the National Press Club', 2 February 2015 (www.liberal.org.au/latest-news/2015/02/02/prime-minister-address-national-press-club).

5. Latika Bourke, 'Joe Hockey's advice to first homebuyers – get a good job that pays good money', *The Sydney Morning Herald*, 9 June 2015 (www.smh.com.au/federal-politics/political-news/joe-hockeys-advice-to-first-homebuyers--get-a-good-job-that-pays-good-money-20150609-ghjqyw.html).

6. 'Job snobs label unfair to unemployed, say Abbott's critics', *7.30 Report*, 1 June 1999, ABC TV (www.abc.net.au/7.30/stories/s27562.htm).

7. Samantha Donovan, 'Indigenous "lifestyle choices" won't close the gap: PM', *AM*, 11 March 2015, ABC Radio (www.abc.net.au/am/content/2015/s4195123.htm).

8. Karl Marx, *Kapital*, vol. 1.

CHAPTER 4: DEBT, DEFICITS AND BUDGET HONESTY

1. Joe Hockey, 'The Case for Change – Address by the Hon. Joe Hockey MP, Treasurer', 23 April 2014 (www.liberal.org.au/latest-news/2014/04/23/case-change-address-hon-joe-hockey-mp-treasurer).

2. National Commission of Audit, 'National Commission of Audit

Releases Review of the Activities of the Commonwealth Government', media release (www.ncoa.gov.au/media-release.html).

3. ABS, 2014, 'Government Financial Estimates, Australia, 2014-15 Final', catalogue number 5501.0.55.001, 18 November 2014 (www.abs.gov.au/AUSSTATS/abs@.nsf/DetailsPage/5501.0.55.0012014-15%20Final?OpenDocument).

4. 'Joe Hockey, Andrew Robb Transcript – Joint doorstop', 2 August 2013 (www.liberal.org.au/latest-news/2013/08/02/joe-hockey-andrew-robb-transcript-joint-doorstop).

5. 'We've fundamentally honoured core commitments" says Tony Abbott', *7.30*, 4 December 2014, ABC TV (www.abc.net.au/7.30/content/2014/s4142593.htm).

6. Joe Hockey on *Q&A*, 19 May 2014, ABC TV (www.abc.net.au/tv/qanda/txt/s3989246.htm).

7. 'Peter Costello slams Abbott tax plan as a "morbid joke"', News.com.au, 14 April 2015 (www.news.com.au/finance/economy/peter-costello-slams-abbott-tax-plan-as-a-morbid-joke/story-fn84fgcm-1227302770409).

8. Paolo Mauro, Rafael Romeu, Ariel Binder & Asad Zaman, 2013, 'A Modern History of Fiscal Prudence and Profligacy', IMF Working Paper, Fiscal Affairs Department (www.imf.org/external/pubs/ft/wp/2013/wp1305.pdf).

9. Catherine McGrath, 'Liberal leak damage', *PM*, ABC Radio, 2 May 2001 (www.abc.net.au/pm/stories/s288187.htm).

10. See Transfield Annual Reports (various years).

11. Unconventional Economist, 'Is the Australian economy recession proof?', *Macro Business*, 10 September 2013 (www.macrobusiness.com.au/2013/09/is-the-australian-economy-recession-proof).

12. In announcing the peak in interest rates of 7.25 per cent in March 2008, the governor of the Reserve Bank, Glenn Stevens, drew attention to the rapid growth in demand, which was outstripping the growth in productive capacity (see www.rba.gov.au/media-releases/2008/mr-08-03.html).

13. Australian Government, 2015, *2015-16 Budget Paper no 1*; RBA, 1996, *Historical Statistics*; and OECD, *General Government* (https://data.oecd.org/gga/general-government-debt.htm).

14. Richard Denniss, 'Joe Hockey's penny-pinching will constrain growth', *The Age*, 27 February 2015 (www.theage.com.au/comment/joe-hockeys-pennypinching-will-constrain-growth-20150227-13qhy9.html).

CHAPTER 5: THE TRUTH ABOUT THE FREE MARKET

1. ABS, 2013, 'Household Energy Consumption Survey, Australia: Summary of Results, 2012', catalogue number 4670.0, 24 September 2013 (www.abs.gov.au/AUSSTATS/abs@. nsf/DetailsPage/4670.02012?OpenDocument); Jim Minifie, 2014, 'Super Sting: how to stop Australians paying too much for superannuation', Grattan Institute Report No. 2014-6.

2. Australian Taxation Office, 2015, 'Income for Medicare levy surcharge, thresholds and rates' (www.ato.gov.au/Individuals/ Medicare-levy/Medicare-levy-surcharge/Income-for-Medicare-levy-surcharge,-thresholds-and-rates).

3. Jared Owens, 'David Leyonhjelm declares war on nanny state', *The Australian*, 26 June 2015 (www.theaustralian.com.au/ national-affairs/david-leyonhjelm-declares-war-on-nanny-state/story-fn59niix-1227415288323?sv=269b8156e7f4031a81 b36975114c4e93).

3. 'Fact Check: Does infrasound from wind farms make people sick?', *Fact Check*, ABC News, 17 July 2015 (www.abc.net.au/ news/2015-07-17/wind-farms-david-leyonhjelm-fact-check/ 6553746).

4. Paul Murrell, 'Changes to car import laws – Part 4', *Practical Motoring*, 5 July 2015 (https://practicalmotoring.com.au/car-news/changes-to-car-import-laws-part-4).

5. Lisa Cox, 'Tony Abbott attacks ANU's "stupid decision" to dump fossil fuel investments', *The Sydney Morning Herald*, 15 October 2014 (www.smh.com.au/federal-politics/political-news/tony-abbott-attacks-anus-stupid-decision-to-dump-fossil-fuel-investments-20141015-116a0y.html).

CHAPTER 6: THE MYTH OF FREE TRADE

1. Productivity Commission (2015) *Trade & Assistance Review 2013–14*, Annual Report Series, Productivity Commission, Canberra (www.pc.gov.au/research/ongoing/trade-assistance/ 2013-14/trade-assistance-review-2013-14.pdf).

2. ABS, 'Australian System of National Accounts, 2014-15', catalogue number 5204.0, 30 October 2015 (www.abs.gov.au/ AUSSTATS/abs@.nsf/MF/5204.0).

3. Alan Bjerga, 'Japan keeps lid on rice, U.S. on sugar in Trans-Pacific deal', *Bloomberg Business*, 6 October 2015 (http://www. bloomberg.com/news/articles/2015-10-05/japan-keeps-lid-on-rice-u-s-on-sugar-in-trans-pacific-deal).

4. Australian Manufacturing Workers' Union, n.d., 'China deal trades away jobs, rights' (http://www.amwu.org.au/china_deal_trades_away_jobs_rights).

5. Australian Fair Trade & Investment Network Ltd, n.d., 'Special rights for foreign investors to sue governments' (http://aftinet.org.au/cms/isds-sue-governments-tpp-2013).

6. Michael Brissenden, 'FTA: "Nothing's agreed until everything's agreed", says trade minister Andrew Robb', *AM*, ABC Radio, 27 July 2015 (www.abc.net.au/am/content/2015/s4281110.htm).

7. 'ABC Radio RN Breakfast – interview with Fran Kelly', transcript, 29 July 2015 (http://trademinister.gov.au/transcripts/Pages/2015/ar_tr_150729.aspx).

CHAPTER 7: THE USE AND ABUSE OF ECONOMIC MODELLING

1. Joseph Stiglitz, 'Information and the Change in the Paradigm in Economics', Nobel Prize Lecture, 8 December 2001 (www.nobelprize.org/nobel_prizes/economic-sciences/laureates/2001/stiglitz-lecture.pdf).

2. Jessica Irvine, 'Increase GST to 15 per cent and broaden to raise $256 billion: accountants', *The Sydney Morning Herald*, 20 July 2015 (www.smh.com.au/nsw/increase-gst-to-15-per-cent-and-broaden-to-raise-256-billion-accountants-20150714-gibmk6.html).

3. Land Court of Queensland, Adani Mining Pty Ltd v Land Services of Coast and Country Inc & Ors [2015] QLC 48.

4. Land and Environment Court of New South Wales, Hunter Environment Lobby inc v Minister for Planning and Infrastructure (no 2).

5. Peter Abelson, 'Establishing a Monetary Value for Lives Saved: Issues and Controversies', WP 2008-02, Office of Best Practice Regulation Department of Finance and Deregulation, Applied Economics and Department of Economics, Sydney University.

6. Katharine Q. Seelye & John Tierney, 'E.P.A. drops age-based cost studies', *The New York Times*, 8 May 2003; Joseph E. Aldy & W. Kip Viscusi, 2007, 'Age Differences in the Value of Statistical Life: Revealed Preference Evidence', *Review of Environmental Economics and Policy*, vol. 1, no. 2, pp. 241–260.

7. Richard Denniss, 'Woolly Figures: An analysis of the Treasury's modelling of emissions from sheep and cattle', Policy Brief No. 4, The Australia Institute, 21 October 2009 (http://www.tai.org.au/node/1574).

Chapter 8: What Can Be Done?

1. Marie-Helene Martin, 'Equality Begins in the Creche', *The Guardian*, 19 February 2010 (www.theguardian.com/commentisfree/2010/feb/19/france-motherhood-childcare-equality).

2. See Tourism Research Australia, 2015, *State Tourism Satellite Accounts 2013-14*, Austrade, Canberra (http://www.tra.gov.au/documents/Economic-Industry/State_Tourism_Satellite_Accounts_2013_14_FINAL.pdf); and ABS, '2011 Census of population and housing' (www.abs.gov.au/websitedbs/censushome.nsf/home/data).

REDBACK QUARTERLY BOOKS WITH BITE

BATTLERS & BILLIONAIRES
THE STORY OF INEQUALITY IN AUSTRALIA
Andrew Leigh

WHY WE ARGUE ABOUT CLIMATE CHANGE
Eric Knight

'Required reading for every Australian who seriously cares about the fair go enduring.'
—Peter FitzSimons

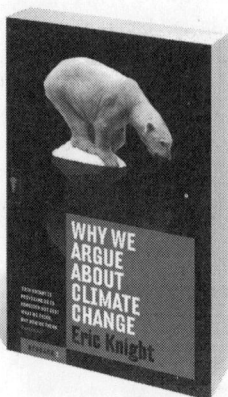

'Eric Knight is provoking us to consider not just what we think, but how we think.'
—Waleed Aly

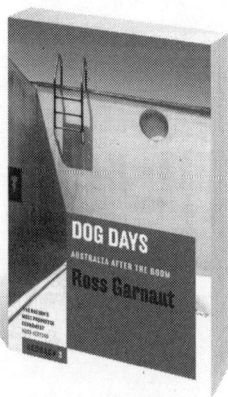

DOG DAYS
AUSTRALIA AFTER THE BOOM
Ross Garnaut

ANZAC'S LONG SHADOW
THE COST OF OUR NATIONAL OBSESSION
James Brown

'This book is a must-read for anyone concerned with the economic and social future of Australia ... lucid, compelling and unburdened by political bias.' —Bob Hawke

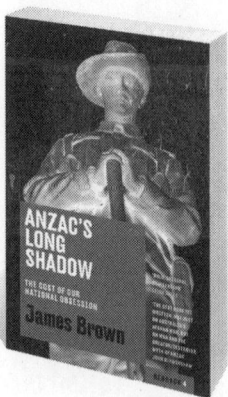

'The best book yet written, not just on Australia's Afghan war, but on war itself and the creator/destroyer myth of Anzac.' —John Birmingham

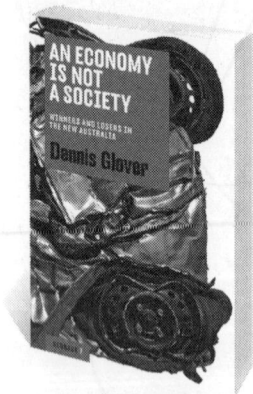